Books by V. S. PRITCHETT

The Offensive Traveller
   (1964)

When My Girl Comes Home
   (1961)

The Sailor, Sense of Humour, and Other Stories
   (1956)

The Spanish Temper
   (1954)

THESE ARE BORZOI BOOKS, PUBLISHED IN NEW YORK
BY ALFRED A. KNOPF

The Offensive Traveller

THE
Offensive Traveller

by V. S. PRITCHETT

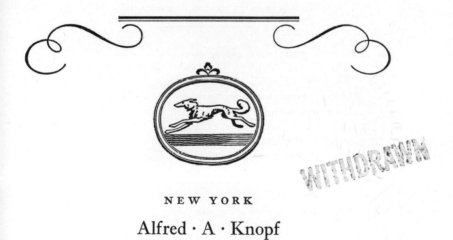

NEW YORK

Alfred · A · Knopf

1964

L. C. catalog card number: 64-19806

THIS IS A BORZOI BOOK,
PUBLISHED BY ALFRED A. KNOPF, INC.

FIRST EDITION

All of the chapters appeared originally in *Holiday*.

Published in England as *Foreign Faces*
by Chatto & Windus, Ltd.

Contents

The Offensive Traveller

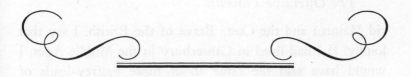

The Offensive Traveller

I am an offensive traveller. I do not mean that I arrive in a foreign country in a state of arrogance and start complaining about the beds, the plumbing, the food, the transport, the prices. I do not refuse to drink the water; I do not see bacteria everywhere. I do not say: "The country is wonderful, but you can have the people." I do not suspect everyone who speaks a foreign language of being a thief. I do not scream that I cannot get a good steak in Morocco —steak travellers are the hypochondriacs of motion—a decent haggis in Naples, or an edible chop suey on Ascension Island. I do not complain of the lack of Night Life in English villages or of the absence of thatch in Ohio. One thing, of course, does annoy me: other tourists. Clear the Americans out of Paris; throw the Germans out of Venice;

3

rid Majorca and the Costa Brava of the British. I say that loudly. If I had lived in Canterbury in the Middle Ages, I would have said the same about those palfrey-loads of pilgrims. To the inhabitants I am as obliging as a Portuguese. By "being offensive" I mean that I travel, therefore I offend. I represent that ancient enemy of all communities: the stranger. Neapolitan girls have crossed themselves to avert the evil eye at the sight of me. (And of you, too, *hypocrite lecteur*.) And rightly: We are looking on the private life of another people, a life which is entirely their business, with an eye that, however friendly it may be, is alien. We are seeing people as they do not see themselves. I say "we," but I do worse than this. I not only look. I make notes. I write.

Forty years ago I wrote my first impressions of a country not my own and began my career as a traveller who causes offence in print. I began to be paid for insulting others. I remember the first occasion. There was—perhaps there still is—a local train that runs from Cork to Blarney (significant destination!) and the country people piled in bringing their chickens with them. I mentioned the fact because the journey was a jolly one in a country then torn apart by Civil War. I was accused of bringing the new Irish nation into ridicule. No Irish man or woman ever brought a chicken into a train. If he or she did, a foreigner ought not to mention it. I was playing up the Victorian charm of a nation determined to be Victorian no longer. I moved on to Spain, where I was accused of saying there would shortly be a vacant throne: there was, but in this my offence was without distinction. Everyone was saying it. Who were my

4

friends? Abominable intellectuals like Unamuno, Ortega y Gasset, Baroja—people who were notorious Europeanizers and objectors to bullfighting and were kindly disposed to education, parliaments, football, and walking in the mountains. I migrated to the United States; my talent developed. One summer evening I was sitting on the jetty of a small New England town listening to the distant voices of some old fellows jawing and whittling away. I could not hear what they said, but on that peaceful evening the sound was like one of the pleasantest sounds in nature: the cawing of returning rooks. I was a fanciful youth. I mentioned the sound in print. Uproar. I had conveyed that New Englanders, among all human animals, had not yet evolved the power of speech, forgetting in my smug British way that English speech has been compared to the hissing of geese.

With this incident, I realized that I had been born with a remarkable gift. I exploited it. There were the Swiss, for example; I praised them for their domestic contentment. They objected at once: did I not know that their family life was as awful as that of any other people? Was I insinuating that they lacked a capacity to suffer? A young Swiss came to my office in London to assure me that a Swiss could suffer, if he got half a chance, as much as any man on earth. I praised Scandinavian architecture. These Nordics were indignant that I had not mentioned their high suicide rate. In time, the Germans spoke out. When I said that the Germans loved flowers I was clearly insinuating that they were "sissies" and one reader got in a nasty dig at me. "Don't the British love flowers too?" The mayor

5

of a town in South America said I obviously intended an affront when I said they had just installed traffic lights. My gift was developing fast—so fast that I was invited to a discussion on the Welsh character in a small Welsh town and there I made the sort of mistake that comes from over-confidence. I was asked to insult the Welsh, because the meeting had fallen into the doldrums of self-praise. The meeting took place in a small room; indeed one of the company, a learned shepherd, had to lie on the floor at my feet. He stared expectantly, waiting to spring. My speech was brief, even trivial. All I said was that the Welsh were touchy, hot-tempered, hypocritical, and given to lying. No more. The shepherd sprang—but not at me. He sprang at the audience and in a beautiful lamenting voice, as if he were declaiming from Jeremiah, he shouted: "What this Englishman has just said is true! We are liars, we are hypocrites . . ."

You observe my error. I learned the lesson and, as a result, reached the peak of my offensive career. It was during the war. I had written a film script showing that the ordinary Englishman and the ordinary Frenchman were natural allies and friends. I presented a flighty and talkative Englishman, keen on beer and girls, and a silent, industrious, abstemious Frenchman, dignified and scrupulous. You notice my cunning? I had reversed a sacred myth. The film was banned as anti-Allied propaganda and insulting to both parties. I could go no higher.

As an offender of foreigners, I recognize that my place in a long tradition is a humble one. Unlike Shakespeare, I have not made fun of foreign accents. I have not made fun

of Frogs, Taffys, Wops, or Polacks. The nonchalance of
Mark Twain and the insinuations of Henry Adams are
far beyond me. Mrs. Trollope being rude to Americans,
Nathaniel Hawthorne being rude about the British, Ber-
nard Shaw making a laughingstock of both, are far above
my level. I could not equal Bemelmans on Ecuador, though
I did get a broadside from a politician in that country—the
eighty volcanoes of the lovely place have, perhaps, con-
tributed to the sensibility of its public men—and I have not
debunked Spain like that brilliant Italian scholar Mario
Praz in *Unromantic Spain*. None of these great offenders
can, of course, vie with Tobias Smollett, whose *Travels
Through France and Italy* is the supreme classic of offence.
Smollett had the fine art of excusing a vice by substituting
a worse one. Of the French he wrote:

> If their acts of generosity are rare, we ought to as-
> cribe that rarity not so much to a deficiency of
> generous sentiments, as to their vanity and ostentation,
> which, engrossing all their funds, utterly disable them
> from exerting the virtues of beneficence.

Taine's view of the British seems to have been that they
were a kind of brute cattle with addled heads and censorious
habits, living in steam. I say nothing of Dr. Johnson and
the Scots. He spoke it at a time when half the inns of
northern England had "Scots go home" chalked on their
walls.

I must not claim too much for my gift for offence. I
could not have been born at a luckier moment. In the

7

eighteenth century it was impossible to offend anyone. Today, more people are offendable than at any other time in the history of the world. The number increases. There are two reasons for this, one of them practical: the other harder to define precisely. The first is that more people travel and annoy one another. People whose blood boiled only once in a lifetime can now have it brought to the boil every night of their lives in books, on television, or in the cinema. Why are they offended? They are rightly offended by errors of fact. But why are personal descriptions and interpretations offensive to them? I think the tendency of modern society is to make us think there ought to be only one view, that there is a mysterious standard eye or opinion like the standard inch. That very unobjective word called "objective" is constantly used. This is natural: we, the offended, are fed on the single view of propaganda, advertising, and myths.

But the second reason for the increase in the number of the offended is more important. More people are offended because more are insecure. More people in the world are uprooted and unsure of themselves. There are more chips on more shoulders. It began with the Industrial Revolution, the break-up of long-settled patterns of life in which people felt so settled that they did not care what was said about them, good or bad. In some countries the Industrial Revolution has only just begun. If I want to stir up chauvinism or hysteria and tickle an inferiority complex, I go to the big cities; the countryman or the man of the small town which has no new buildings cannot easily be moved. A fisherman, a Spanish shepherd, a German woodcutter, a man working in the fields, regards the people who write about him or interpret him with amusement, contentment, and even pity. He is strong in his own world and often better educated, in the true sense of being able to draw on stored experience, than those who have merely new knowledge. But in the new countries and new towns it is not so. Doubt is much stronger. "What do you think of our new telegraph poles?" a Japanese student asked an English poet who was teaching him Gray's "Elegy." The greatest tact was required in the poet's reply. It is offensive in such places not to mention the latest thing. The enormously high buildings shooting up in some unlikely parts of the world may be monuments to modern art, hope, and endeavour; they are also monuments to an inferiority complex. The newer the country the more noticeable the chip, the more certain the aggression. Even when the assured do not condescend to the ill-assured, it is resented that the assured do not know that they are assured. If two assured well-rooted peoples meet—the French and the Spaniards, for example—the comedy has the most delicate dryness, though as far as offence is concerned the French easily win. I have found mayors the most ready of all people to take offence, if their towns are small. A new country or regime regards interpretation or criticism—anything except the official view—as anti-social. And some countries are not as old as they think they are. The Germans are an ancient race; their influence on European institutions has been enormous from the time of the Roman Empire. They are pre-eminent in modern science. They have great vitality and often combine an extraordinary precision in work with a powerful, if not

9

always determinable, emotional force. Everyone has observed this. But as a nation, the Germans are very young. They are, like the young, affronted if their estimate of themselves is questioned. And when Germans, or British, or Italians, or any other people become racial minorities in other countries, they become more chauvinist, more resentful of criticism or interpretation, than their relatives in the homeland. The Italians in Buenos Aires, the British in Chile, the Irish in Sydney or New York, are far thinner-skinned than the people they have left behind. Self-criticism is the beginning of maturity. One of the harshest books ever written by a foreigner about another country was George Borrow's *The Bible in Spain*. It was translated into Spanish about thirty years ago, and was praised by most of the Spanish critics because they recognized in Borrow a fanatical enemy, a man who, they said, might have been one of themselves and not a Bible-punching heretic. They disagreed with every word he wrote. What they admired was his intolerance.

More offence is caused by praise than blame. The Spaniards hate being called romantic by the French, the Irish hate being called fanciful, the British hate being called solid, the French hate being called volatile, the Italians hate being called clever, and the Portuguese dislike being praised for anything at all and quickly tell you how all "your" things are better than theirs. What really offends is the destruction of a myth. I remember Alberto Moravia saying that a young Neapolitan saves up enough money to buy a Vespa in order to dash across Europe to Scandinavia, where (he has been told) passionate, aristocratic girls of surpassing intelligence and beauty are dedicated to free love; while at the same moment, young love-starved Scandinavians are dashing south to Naples, where (they understand) the dark beauties of the South will come out of palaces into their arms. Both parties would clearly be happier in puritan London, where—Billy Graham tells us—the parks are one vast bedroom. It is hard to decide here who are the offended parties. The best thing to do is to declare all parties undersexed. That causes enormous offence. Northern Italians have been saying this successfully of Southern Italians for generations. There are other myths: that Americans talk of nothing but dollars, that the British are strangled by their class system, that the Germans don't laugh, that every Frenchman keeps a mistress, that the South Americans are always shooting each other.

Being an offender, I am myself easily offended. Where is my weak spot? There is no single place. I am a weak spot all over. I just dislike being looked at. As the coachload of tourists passes me with their cameras in my own country, I feel myself swelling into one fevered wound. Has it come to this, I say, as their cameras click, that I have degenerated into a native, a local character daubed with racial characteristics, liable to remind people of what they have read, interesting for my folk customs, my peculiar diet, my curious clothes? Am I being taken for a Dickensian porter, a lord, Mrs. Grundy's husband, a slippery pickpocket, a town crier, a folk dancer, a decayed Empire builder? Or much worse, the supreme insult in fact: am I being studied as an example of the typical? Is someone going home to write about my habits and deduce from them the unlucky attributes of my nation? If you catch me, I am tempted to say, I shall have my revenge. I shall do as I have been done by in many, many countries. I shall be a most misleading guide.

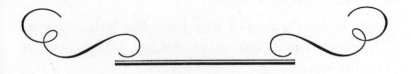

CZECHOSLOVAKIA

We had just landed at Prague Airport.
"Tovarish So-and-So! Tovarish Somebody Else!
Mr. Thompson! Monsieur Le Brun! Herr Schneider!"—
at intervals the girl in the khaki uniform sang out our names
from the window of the Passport Control in a high, sweetish voice. Slaves of anxiety, the Czechs give Communists
and Capitalists their correct titles. I had travelled in a
Czech plane from London; among the passengers were a
dozen spick-and-span Czech school children; and now the
hot, glum little hall of the airport with the inevitable show-
cases of peasant knickknacks was piled with men in jerseys
and open-necked shirts, carrying briefcases and bundles. A
local plane from Bratislava, on the Hungarian border, had
just come in. Lanky or burly, the men wore brown berets,

which sat on the tops of their heads like little puddings. These men looked like people off the land or out of factories.

This was my first journey to a country behind the Iron Curtain. We had flown out of the flash and wealth of Brussels, over the neat red-and-white towns of Germany, and knew we were over Czechoslovakia when the blobs of forest thickened and the villages and towns were straggling and grey-roofed. The Curtain is as much a curtain of words as of iron, for there were no Western periodicals on the plane. (The authorities do not mind the Westerner bringing in his own newspapers, but he will never be able to buy them in Czechoslovakia. The only ones he can buy are *The London Daily Worker*, *L'Humanité*, and *L'Unità*.) One had been told that the customs and currency-control system were severe, but this turned out not to be so. My luggage was not opened. There were customs officers who spoke German, French, English, and Russian, and I have no doubt they could have rustled up a Chinese-speaker, for Chinese was (at that time) the new language snobbery in the satellite countries. I got my money from a clerk who seemed to know London as well as I did. We even talked about the weather. For at that moment a thunderstorm broke. The Czechs put on their mass-produced plastic raincoats; we packed into a shabby bus, bulged in our seats, and splashed our way through the cement-coloured suburbs, across the wide, curving river into Prague. "One of the most beautiful capitals in Europe; provincial since 1914; *kaput* since Hitler's war," a Czech friend had said in London. Was that what I would find?

Central Europe was unknown to me before the war. Of Czechoslovakia since 1947 I knew only the story of the Czech and Polish dogs. They had met at the frontier. The Polish dog was going to Czechoslovakia, he said, to get something to eat. The Czech dog said he was going to Poland because he wanted to bark. After Romania, Czechoslovakia lived under the most rigid of the Communist regimes until 1963. I was there in '61. But the hotels of Prague are full of Western tourists, as well as Russian, North Korean, East German, Hungarian, and Polish visitors; among the businessmen one finds Turks calling up Istanbul, one finds Egyptians calling Cairo and Indians sending cables about cotton and machinery to Bombay, Americans, Argentines, West Germans, and British. A large number of American Czechs come to visit their relatives. Czechoslovakia is an industrial country envied by all the other satellites, for it has a big start in the race for economic self-sufficiency. Since the slight thaw of 1956, when the Czech students protested against Stalinism, and since the discovery that the tourist industry pays handsomely, I don't think that much check is kept on the ordinary traveller. The tourist is certainly not followed or shadowed. But two journalists who had driven in from Poland that evening asked: "What's happening here? We've been given the full treatment: we were followed all the way from the frontier." One has no need of a guide; indeed guides are as hard to come by in the summer as motorcars are. It is true that the Czechs are a little puzzled by a traveller who does not belong to a coach party, a conference, or a trades-union group. One is treated with awe and respect if one is alone, for one represents Western Currency in its most reckless form. To be a writer is also something. Writers have always had enormous prestige in Central Europe, and Communism is a book religion.

One of my first impressions of the Czechs did not change, and indeed was enhanced. They are exceptionally concerned to help and to be kind to strangers. Are you happy? Can I take you to the bus or get you a taxi? Are you worrying about anything? Were you happy yesterday afternoon? Are you sure being alone does not give you *Angst?* What can they do? Have you any complaints? Do you want another pillow? This eagerness to oblige is a characteristic of small countries whose language no foreigner can be expected to speak; but with the Czechs, as with the Portuguese, the need to oblige rises out of a deep and curious national craving. Throughout their history they have craved for help from friends; they long to be loved. I met a good many Czechs—especially Party members—who spoke of the Czechs' "inferiority complex" and who feared that this sensibility to others had gone to the length of neurosis and had turned them into lackeys of international acquaintance. They are a morbidly cautious race surrounded by more spirited peoples. History has trapped them.

Sitting over a glass of Pilsener, I used to speculate about this as I watched the crowds go by in the wide Wenceslaus Square, the Václavské náměstí, the principal street of the city. They belonged to the most prosperous, the most bourgeois of the five satellite states. Heavy beer drinkers, like the Germans, the passers-by were in the main a weighty, broad-shouldered, healthy, solid people, with square-cut jaws, and a great many had the fine, widely set fair blue eyes of the Slavonic races. The thin ones looked brisk and keen. Here was a nation brought up on plain food, beer, pork, dumplings, and sauerkraut, where handsome youth is brief and thickens quickly into worried middle age. They did not dress well; nor did they seem to care. If one saw a well-dressed person, man or woman, it turned out that they were foreigners—East Germans, Argentines, or elderly American ladies. The most striking group in Prague were three or four beautifully dressed men and women from the French Cameroons—Kings and Queens, I do not doubt, who carried themselves with a distinction that showed up the drabness of the city. (They had come to study Czech co-operatives.) Eastern Europe is inelegant. It has become puritan. Elegance is a sin of the corrupt past and the decadent West, and although it is true that the Belgians—with whom the Czechs are often compared—are far from being the best-dressed people in Europe, one glance at the Brussels crowd packing the stations in the rush hour will show the enormous difference in wealth and style between average West and average East.

Yet if the crowd puts use before elegance, if the old smart hotels and restaurants are now grubby and slack, there are many signs of a new, bright popular life. Prague was always a city of small restaurants; it now has its popular up-to-date cafeterias and snack bars. There are dishes of the famous Prague ham, there are galantines, the salmon and lobster aspics, the herrings, anchovies, and eggs in mayonnaise. These places are always packed. Large numbers of married women earn their living in offices and factories, and families go out to eat. There are no luxury shops; the jewelry is poor, and so are the perfumes and cosmetics; women's handbags and shoes are shoddy, mass-produced, and out of fashion. Heels are low. It is incredible, but Russian women queue up in Moscow for Czech shoes! There are innumerable good bookshops, with the usual stress on the European classics, which have a large sale; modern foreign literature appears erratically—the students protested in May 1956 against the prohibitory index of foreign authors—one can get, for example, a Kingsley Amis, Hemingway and Faulkner and Steinbeck, and Graham Greene's *Quiet American*, but not his best work. There are no books by the Czech émigrés. The average Czech wants his radio, his television set, and his modern kitchen equipment, and these are becoming plentiful. The shops of Prague and all Czechoslovakia are better stocked than the shops of any other Eastern European country, but they cannot compete with Düsseldorf. A more dramatic difference is the relative lack of traffic in Prague. One does not hear the warm hammering and droning of a modern city by day or night. By night Prague is still, and footsteps sound a long way off in the streets. On my first night in Prague I even thought there were no cars at all. It was a Sunday, and there is a regulation that officials must not use their cars at the weekend. Later, I saw there were a certain number of cars about, though never enough to make a traffic jam; they trickled by sparsely in twos and threes and I got careless about crossing the Wenceslaus Square. By ten o'clock at night the traffic lights went out and one heard that lonely, delightful, old-fashioned sound of the last trams miauling at the corners of the streets of the old town, under the trees by the river. Prague goes to bed very early and gets up early too. Like the Germans, the Czechs work hard for long hours. You eat to live; you live to work; you work till you sleep; you wake up to work. This is not a pleasure-loving people.

I used to walk down through beautiful old Prague, and stand on the Charles Bridge among the dramatic and mournful religious statues which line its balustrades, and listen to the river going over the low weir and to the quacking of the ducks. I would stand on the bridge trying to get Czechoslovakia into my mind. In Prague one is pretty well at the dead centre of Europe, in one of its historically stormy cities, 750 miles from London, 846 miles from Rome, nearly 1,400 from Athens, and 1,600 from Moscow. The country is shut in by mountains on all sides. It has no sea-coast—except the one invented by Shakespeare: in *A Winter's Tale*, "a desert country near the sea." Its northern frontier is entirely Polish. In the west it runs with East Germany and West Germany; on the south it is bound by Austria; at Bratislava it has a common frontier with Hungary, and in Slovakia its borders run for fifty miles with the Ukraine. It is a country about the size of the state of New York, with a density of population just above the European average—that is to say, about 300 to the square mile. One quarter of the thirteen million Czechoslovaks are Slovaks who live in the eastern part of the country. The population is rising, but since 1939 there has been a loss of nearly two and a half million people due to the expulsion of the Germans from the western end. One hundred and forty thousand Czechs died in German concentration camps, but, on the whole, Czechoslovakia did not suffer severely in the war. I believe only one bomb fell on Prague: the smart new Jalta Hotel stands on the site. One has to imagine a country which is one of the most heavily forested countries in Europe and in which almost every village (in the Czech provinces) has a factory chimney. Except for peasant Slovakia, it is an industrial country, and with such success in recent years in building up its heavy industry that the land has been depleted of agricultural labour. The Czechs now have to import food.

Below the weir silent couples sitting in anchored boats were fishing. In the parks couples sat modestly, occasionally holding hands. Across the river the narrow cobbled hill and arcaded streets of old Prague rose to the Gothic cathedral, massive, grey-and-gold glinting, against the evening sky. Farther over and downstream on Letna Hill rose the appalling granite blob of the Stalin Monument, a crude group of giant figures who seem to be marching down on the city to master it by sheer ugliness and force. All over Eastern Europe such gross and commonplace monuments to the Russian liberation were built in the Stalin period.

How do you explain—I asked my friend L——, a young Party member who had become a Communist after four years in Buchenwald and other concentration camps—how do you explain that a country so advanced technically as Czechoslovakia, so middle-class, could so easily become Communist? It is the only place where Marxist prophecy has proved correct: that Communism would come to the industrialized countries first. "It is very simple," he said.

"The Germans and the Viennese had been for centuries the tyrants against whom the Czechs had had to struggle. The Russians were our liberators, whereas in Poland, historically, they were oppressors. All Czechs speak a little German because of the Occupation and because of trade, but all Czechs can understand Russian without having to learn it because of similarities in the languages. We are in the centre of all the pressures, we have developed, through centuries of oppression, a sharp and subtle political intelligence. The Czechs think and talk abstract politics all day long and have traditionally thrown up acute political leaders inside Czechoslovakia, and outside it when they have emigrated. There was no *sudden* conversion," he said. "When the Czech state was founded in 1918, it already had strong socialist leanings; this was the only country in Central Europe," he said, "where the Party was allowed to operate legally all the time between the wars. The great land-owners were foreigners and disappeared in 1918, so we had no feudal problems; the owners of the great industries were, very often, collaborators with the Nazis (the accusation that 'all Czechs collaborated' is common in Eastern Europe); we had already before 1939 a Czech Catholic Church, so that little stood in our way."

He was an educated man of middle-class background, in his late thirties, who knew France, Britain, and the United States. In a worried way he regretted the loss of some personal freedoms, but was convinced that these were coming back. He would not yield an inch, however, about the necessity of keeping the Western press from public sale. He spoke vaguely and cautiously of "the mistakes" that had been made and "the crimes" that had been committed under Stalinism, saying that he had been in a position to know more than most people and could say nothing at the time. All Czechs are irritated by the extreme difficulty—amounting to a ban—of travel in the West, but he thought the difficulties were lessening. At any rate, one could usually get a visa to visit relatives at Vienna, which is regarded as paradise, especially because of the opera.

Knowing that at the time of the May Day celebrations in 1956, the university students had presented a resolution to the Party's Central Committee calling, among other things, for less adulation of the Soviet Union and asking questions about the ownership and management of the Jáchymov mines and uranium resources—the product goes to Russia—I asked him why the protests in Czechoslovakia in 1956 had been less violent than those of Hungary and Poland.

"We always do things more quietly. We are cautious. We change without fuss," he repeated. "You must remember that the Russians were the historic enemies of Hungary and Poland in the old days, whereas the Russians were historically our friends." The fact is that in 1940, in 1948, and in 1956 the Czechs waited to see how the cat would jump.

Foreigners generally say that 90 per cent of the people are opposed to the regime. Naturally, this speaker did not agree. He said a majority of the older generation might be against it, but they had been made powerless; and that, by now, a younger generation who knew nothing else accepted it entirely. (This is not borne out by the student's protest.) It is general Eastern European propaganda—it comes up in conversation everywhere with all sorts of people—that the East Germans are now as thoroughly indoctrinated as themselves. Since the building of the wall in Berlin, this seems to be untrue of the East Germans.

I have summarized L——'s views and no doubt I have simplified them. In his remarks about the Church this man did not, for example, mention that 43 per cent of the priests had been deprived of their parishes; but he was right in conveying that the Czechs had been in dispute with the Vatican from 1918 onwards and that the fight had not been purely a Communist interest.

Prague, or more particularly old Prague, which is very large, is one of the noblest cities in Europe. Its hundred Gothic spires prick the sky; its medieval towers, its Baroque belfries and cupolas, bring their graces to the city panorama. One has an impression of another Paris of the Latin Quarter. The broad river curves through the tree-lined embankments. One can see by the war between Gothic and Baroque that this city is marked at every corner by historical political struggle. It is a difficulty for the Czech to admire the Baroque because it is the architecture of a foreign conqueror, though some of the art historians are beginning to weaken and point out that it was also the work of Czech artisans. One could see why L—— claimed that the Czechs had the highest level of political education in Europe; they have learned in the bitter school of oppression.

It was what they call "the cucumber season" when I was in Prague, the time when the opera is closed and there are no new plays and films. Everyone who can, gets away to

23

the fifty-mile stretch of the Danube, to the Tatra Mountains and the beautiful towns of wild, wine-drinking Slovakia. Coachloads of tourists, some of them American, but chiefly East and West Germans, come in. There was a load or two of North Koreans.

I spent a lot of time wandering about old Prague, diving into those arcades that lead from street to street, or into those alleys that tunnel under the old houses, open into courtyards, and disappear under the houses again. An ingenious walker can cross a good deal of old Prague under cover. On the steep, cobbled hill that goes up to the cathedral, there is a maze that eventually climbs by alleys, by steps, and even by what seem to be private doorways and tunnels, to a pretty open-air restaurant on a ledge overlooking the city, where one might be at Saint Germain-en-Laye looking across to Paris. The Well of Gold is one of the two or three little restaurants in the old part of the city where the food is good, if in the heavy German style, and where the service is passable. Prague does not escape the general blight on catering that has spread from Russia. In the larger restaurants, waiters are few, amateur, negligent, and slow. To be thirsting for a glass of beer in one of the large places is misery. A customer at the Hofbräuhaus, the well-known popular beerhall in Munich, has hardly sat down before he is served even when the enormous place is packed and roaring; but at Flecu, the equally famous old-style beer garden in Prague, the traditional resort of all Czechs who take their beer drinking seriously, one can sit for half an hour before the puffing wench comes round carrying a dozen heavy pint pots of beer shoulder-high on her tray. And Czechs do not stop at a pint. Half a dozen is modest. The waiter or waitress is usually not allowed to accept money, and there is one more waiting period before one can catch the wandering cashier. In many respects Communism has revived the old Austro-Hungarian bureaucratic habits; the waiters are caught up in some chit-filling system; the manager—who may be the original owner of the restaurant or one transferred from a place of his own, in order to cure him of proprietorial "errors"—has lost his authority. He is simply the representative of the restaurant keepers' co-operative. But, I was told, the running of restaurants had greatly improved since the early days of Communism, when the profit target had been put too high. The disheartened manager would increase his sales of spirits in order to reach the figure quickly; the result was a serious rise of alcoholism, and the State had to put a very high price on spirits in order to reduce the sale. Now that many restaurants have reverted to management by old owners, they are better run; but it is wiser to choose the small ones, which are anxious to show the Westerner that they haven't forgotten what a good place ought to be.

It is quite untrue that the Czechs fear to talk to strangers; but it is not in their nature to talk incautiously. I used often to walk across the Charles Bridge to a passable tavern and have lunch at a long table with a cheerful and noisy lot of carpenters, plumbers, building labourers, and clerks, who talked about their jobs, about fishing in the river and football. They ate out because their wives were working. The Voice of America used to come over the radio. No one talked politics—that never happens unless

25

one is alone with someone. It is true, again, that few Czechs will invite a foreigner to their homes, and although this may have something to do with caution, it is also due to embarrassment. Houses and flats are crowded and split up because of the chronic housing shortage.

"We have concentrated on building factories," is one explanation of this. The other is the general movement of population from the land to the cities.

Among the builders was a strange, gracious, lonely man who took me to his flat. Like many Czechs of his age, he had been to Belgium and France after 1930, during the slump, looking for work. Life had battered him. He looked twenty years older than he really was. *"La vie difficile,"* he said bleakly. He and his wife—she was in hospital at the time—lived in a two-room flat in one of the old, pretty streets by the river where the millrace runs and the boys play; two rooms being the official allowance of space. The flat was like many one sees in the Latin Quarter in Paris, and the rooms were made pretty in the Central European manner by indoor plants and peasant coverings on the divans. We had gone there because he could not stand the bad coffee at the restaurant and wanted to make Turkish coffee at home. This man paid a 1939 rent for his flat, and he said that all through Czechoslovakia rents had been kept at this level and were "incredibly low." This is true of all Eastern European states. He agreed that they were too low to cover the cost of repairs. This man's only complaint was that of all Czechs: boredom, the virtual impossibility of travelling to the West.

"I can go to Poland and Hungary for my holidays very

26

cheaply. I can go to Bulgaria and the Black Sea. But all these countries are the same: they bore me. I want to see something different."

Like the British in the austerity period after the war, he felt a craving for pleasure, for the luxuries and plenty of life such as the British saw, in those days, in countries like Switzerland. He also had the Czech craving for a sight of the Adriatic and the Mediterranean, which are closed to them. He was not a Communist—the Party is jealously kept small in all these countries—but his political opinions were a mixture of acquiescence and a nostalgia for the period between the wars. This came out in the common reproach that the British had "lost interest" in Central Europe; if they had been firm before the war and afterwards, the present situation would not exist; and in his bitter conviction that the Americans were backing the Germans and reviving the old German aggression, in which Czechoslovakia would be the first, the traditional sufferer, as it had always been. There is little spirit of rebellion. Like all Czechs, he was a keen questioner about Western politics and very acute in argument, but he was extremely surprised to hear that West Germany was far more prosperous than East Germany!

We went out to look at the old houses in the street called Neruda, with the carved signs of trade or family over the door—the stone key or the wheel—and looked at a few churches. He pointed out, with the builder's expert eye and distaste, the places where the marble was faked or where the carved cherubs had been replaced by copies. We sat under the acacias on the terrace of a little café up by the superb piece of Baroque pride, the Černin Palace (now the Foreign Ministry). We went out to the heights of old Prague, with its quiet places of fine buildings and graceful gardens and parklike woods. We watched the buzzing wasps; we listened to the chatter of very genteel old ladies in their best, drinking their coffee and eating their chocolate cake; we heard the sound of a sculptor's chisel as he chipped away at the statue of an angel in the doorway of a church down the road.

The motorbikes with their girl pillion riders occasionally roared by: we walked down to the old square, where motor coaches unloaded a lot of Slovak girls in short, bunched-out peasant skirts—the peasant dresses are very fine, and the girls have a full, placid beauty; young men clicked their cameras getting pictures of arcades and old towers. Old men sat reading papers in the café. Later on, teen-agers—a local problem—were bawling at a street corner. One evening I saw about six hundred of these youngsters at a café concert, in their liveliest clothes, drinking wine, eating, and listening to popular singers and an orchestra. They were spirited and gay. But the popular songs from the West are terribly out of date. One or two youths went onto the platform and sang songs like "Sentimental Johnny" and "Sonny Boy." They sang in English. As far as they were concerned, the popular culture of the West stopped twenty or thirty years ago. They rarely see an American, French, or British film; if they do, it is always very old. On the other hand, modern Italian films are shown everywhere, even in very small towns. The best Czech films are the brilliant cartoons. One has the impression of great

originality about to burst out, if only artists could be freed
from political clichés, for the theatre is a traditional passion among the masses of this country.

To see the working crowd unbuttoned and enjoying
itself, I decided to go to Bratislava. I got a seat on one of
those crowded little planes that fly seven times a day, except Sundays, from Prague. One is flying out of Bohemia,
southeastwards to the Danube at the point where Austria
and Hungary and·Czechslovakia meet. It is a flight over
high, forested country, towards the plain of the Danube.
There the air is soft and warm, for Czechoslovakia is a
country with a number of very different pockets of climate.
Bratislava is the capital of Slovakia. Historically it has
always been an important military and trading town from
the time of the Romans. It has known occupation by Slavs,
Tartars, Turks, Magyars, and Germans—Hungary still
regards it as Hungarian—and it was badly smashed up in
the last war. The Russians liberated it and rebuilt the massive railway bridge across the wide, fast-flowing river, and
now it is a modern industrial town. Its factories and new
housing estates spread out along the plain.

This region is the most attractive part of the whole
country to the traveller. Its towns have all the beauty that
grows out of an old aristocratic culture. Slovakia is rural,
backward in education, very Catholic, difficult politically
—the peasants dislike the collective or co-operative farm.
I used to see an old peasant woman standing in a doorway
in Prague selling Slovak cheese; a sly official in the
Foreign Ministry said she was "probably the only unsocialized trader left in the city." In Slovakia the Party has

often been in trouble in its attempt to introduce industries, kill illiteracy, and raise the standard of living. The Slovak has nothing Germanic in him. He is a wine drinker, excitable and independent.

The town was packed out, mainly with sun-reddened holiday-making workers, when I was there. Motor coaches packed into the main square, bringing thousands from East Germany, Hungary, and Bulgaria. There were parties filing a hundred at a time into the huge cafés and restaurants and hotels, filling up with beer and wine, dancing in the hotels, and celebrating the Eastern International bicycle races. One of the sights of travel in these parts is the handsome blue Bulgarian six-wheeler trucks and the good-looking young men and women who drive them. Only the Polish travellers looked poor. The riverbank opposite the city was littered with globular sunbathers. There was dancing. There was a small fair. Hundreds of motorbikes and quite a few cars were parked under the trees, and up and down the Danube went the smart white pleasure steamers. There was nothing of Coney Island or Blackpool in Bratislava. Its amusements were homely. A few people went to see the pictures in the historical exhibition of Czech and Polish painting. (It contained some excellent eighteenth-century pictures from Poland.) Most of the crowd wandered into the vegetable and fruit market or listened to the military tunes played by a worker's band in the square. A travelling exhibition coach from East Germany did a heavy trade in foreign stamps—stamp collecting is a craze in all these countries; most post offices have a philatelic department—and it was hard to get a seat among the crowd in the café of the best hotel, and harder still to get a glass of beer in the cheap open-air cafés under the chestnut trees.

There is a Gypsyish, Hungarian side to life in Bratislava. There are some quarters of lazy Hungarian poverty, where swarthy mothers chase half-naked children down the street. The crowd walked slowly up and down the promenade by the Danube, the girls sat decorously on the benches; youths sat on the walls, whistling and shouting to attract the girls. The great event was the start and the finish of the international bicycle race. A good number of rural holiday makers had turned up in their peasant dress. One saw men in short black-and-white embroidered jackets, white shirts, and white linen trousers, or in long soft Russian boots, and wearing broad red-and-green sashes— these last, Bulgarians. One or two of the heroic cyclists lay on the ground and had an exhibitionist massage; a procession of school girls turned up with bouquets of flowers for the starters, who, when the race began, threw them to the crowd. No cheers, no shouts, but general hand clapping.

Meals at Bratislava were good, due to Hungarian influence and the Moravian wine, but I had a curious experience in the packed hotel one lunchtime. I shared a table with an explosive businessman from Beirut who had spent several months in Czechoslovakia, and who had with him a young Czech engineer. We were at once caught by persecution mania. Mr. Beirut was a loud-voiced man who shouted to his friend: "Every hotel has its spies. I bet they'll break up this party: one Czech talking to two foreigners! Especially with me. I never mince matters. I tell everyone what I think."

He certainly did, as loudly as possible. Almost at once, a

waiter tapped the Czech on the shoulder and said he was wanted on the telephone.

"What did I tell you!" exclaimed Mr. Beirut. "The telephone trick. They've made enquiries and are warning him already."

The young man came back.

"Well," said Mr. Beirut, "who was the call from?"

"From my home," said the young man.

"You are sure it wasn't from your 'other home'?" suggested Mr. Beirut. "Who spoke to you? Your father?"

"My grandfather," said the young man simply.

"But he is in bed ill, you told me."

"He is better," said the young man with a smile.

Czechs are very deep. I think there was nothing in it, and that Mr. Beirut was just showing off. We had a long, pleasant lunch. We argued about everything. We even argued about whether Tolstoy's *Resurrection*, his last novel, was an "optimistic" or a "pessimistic" work: an important point, because Czech writers are directed to have an optimistic outlook. More important, when I said that to judge by the crowd, Bratislava was a totally working-class city, the young Czech shook his head. Only 5 per cent of the large middle class were visible, he said. The rest had taken protective colouring and had pretended to merge—which must be true, when one considers that tens of thousands of professional men, shopkeepers, and the so-called "village rich" were deprived of their living at the time of the revolution.

The young man had the sly, quiet, ironical manner of many Czechs. He came, he said, from a "suspect social background," for his father had been a lawyer. The father had been thrown out of his job in the revolution, and had become a waiter, a hotel porter, and so on, and had at last gone in for the making of musical instruments. "In fact, it is an old hobby of his and he is very happy in it and he makes a little money."

"But your prospects aren't very good," shouted Mr. Beirut.

"Well, no," said the young Czech. "I am very poorly paid and I shan't get promotion for a long time. One has to be patient. I know I would be far better off in West Germany, or anywhere at all outside Eastern Europe."

He had been lucky to be allowed to go to the university. There are tens of thousands of Czechs who have been victimized as far as higher education is concerned by political policy. When I was back in Prague I asked my Party friend about this. He did not deny the young engineer's story, but said, as he always did, that it was less likely to happen since 1956 and that the regime was liberalizing itself. But there was another side to it (he said). Not only in Czechoslovakia, but in Central Europe generally, the ambition of middle-class families was to get their sons into the liberal professions and the bureaucracy, which had always been overcrowded. It was a middle-class vice. Nowadays, the government diverted students from overcrowded faculties, and the overcrowded ones were those in which the ex-bourgeois were often most numerous. He agreed that, all things being equal, the preference and freedom of choice went to the labourers' and factory workers' sons.

In a large number of Bohemian and Slovak towns, the

traveller finds lovely examples of Baroque and Gothic architecture, delicate wall paintings and carving, and the country has always been famous for its medicinal spas. Such attractive things are carefully preserved. The roads are not disfigured by billboards; advertising can be said not to exist. In this respect, Eastern Europe is soothing. One is never pestered by touts and cheats and those who prey upon the tourist. Bills are honest, and when foreigners give tips, the Czechs accept them with a pleasant sense of nostalgia for old sins, for Czechs themselves rarely tip.

Leaning on the wall of the Charles Bridge in Prague, I watched the broad river, the Vltava, slowly flowing over the weirs northward toward the vineyards of Mělník. There the Elbe joins it and cuts through the narrow break into the hills to Dresden across the frontier. Except for the Vltava Valley and the valleys that open southeast from Brno or Gottwaldov (the shoemaking town) in Moravia down to the plain of the Danube, Czechoslovakia is a high plateau broken into hummocks, hills, cliffs, ravines, and mountains. To get out of Prague west or south the train has to climb. It is a country of trees, of dark firs, speckled birches, the oak, the ash, and the chestnut. Even in the outskirts of Prague, in the wide, rolling stretches of grain-bearing land, where the rivers are slow and the lakes are still, the horizon always closes in little woods or long, deep parades of forest. I took the train out to Kutná Hora, a town of fourteen thousand inhabitants, which lies an hour and a half to the east. There was an amusing racing-car mechanic in my compartment, one of those droll, laughing-and-winking, energetic young Czechs who often seem to have a touch of the Irish countryman about them. He put on a naïve manner as he joked about not being allowed to go to the big Western motor races, such as Le Mans or Monte Carlo. The Czechs have had a long training under the Austrian Empire in the art of playing the simpelton in order to hide their thoughts. Someone else came into the compartment, and the mechanic stopped talking at once, but every now and then he gave me a wink and a childlike grin. No one spoke for the rest of the journey. He got out at some wayside place, a village of bungalows where the gardens were hot with flowers. I saw him walking off with the dreamy, smiling look of misleading naïveté on his eager face.

The country on the way to Kutná Hora was mild and green, changing from cornland to hills, from hills to long watery stretches of birch and fir; but it is a landscape of surprises. The spotless station at Kutná Hora stands near a large factory where the vale is wide, but the dusty road up from the station climbs and climbs until you find yourself in the classical small Bohemian town, on the edge of a dramatic rocky ravine, where the sunny woods hang down richly over a river. From the top you see a countryside chopped into hills. It is the region of the silver mines which enriched the kings of Bohemia even before the seventeenth century. In the fine Gothic cathedral, in what must have been the citadel, there is a strange statue, painted in the Baroque style, of a silver miner with imploring eyes, holding his lamp. He makes a startling emotional appearance among the saints and angels. I arrived late in the afternoon, when the sun was slanting through the trees and few people were about. They were working in the fields or the factory. The hotel was one of those dingy old places where provincial salesmen would stay in the old days, with the wide stone passageway and the enormous whitewashed and vaulted kitchen of stagecoach times. I have seen many kitchens like this in Czechoslovakia. They belong, by nature, to the stone buildings and the arcaded streets of older Bohemia and give the country its character. The hotel was simple, bare, and clean; the rooms were immensely high. You climb long flights of stone stairs. The great iron wood-burning stove in the bedroom reminds the traveller that the winters of Czechoslovakia are severe. I passed a goodish night there on a mattress filled, I guessed, with wood shavings or lump straw. I thought I was sleeping on mice.

A very old woman seemed to run the hotel, and I imagined it was deserted. I was wrong. By six o'clock two large dining rooms were full of local people and remained so until nearly midnight. The following day, fifty young children from a nursery school came in for lunch with their teachers. Since the State obliges the married women to work outside the home, men, women, and children eat out where and when they can. Every day you notice more and more instances of group life. The restaurant was unlike the Prague restaurant, in one respect: the waiters rushed about in the old capitalist manner. Pint after pint of beer, trayloads of it, appeared at once on the tables, followed by those large plates of veal or kidney soup which are regarded as the absolute necessities of life.

There were only a few shops in Kutná Hora: a draper's,

a yarn shop, a newspaper shop, a place for pots and pans, a pharmacy—I don't know by what freak of circumstance it had a bottle of Chanel 5 in its window. It must have been there before the Communists took over and trade with the West dwindled, and it was the only bottle of French perfume I saw in weeks of travel from Warsaw to the Black Sea. One tiny shop had a window filled with the photographs of dogs, and I suddenly realized I had seen hardly any dogs in the country. It turned out that the Czechs rarely keep them, and certainly never keep a mongrel. If they have a dog, it must be of the finest breed, and this little shopwindow was really a canine beauty show.

The country buses pulled in and a couple of international buses brought in parties of visiting workers from Poland and Hungary and a load of children who had come to see the famous cathedral. In the market square a single stall was set out; it sold yellow and green mushrooms of many varieties. Among the mushroom, sauerkraut, cucumber, and yellow pepper, the Czech cook passes his life and, meat being short this summer, people filled up on potatoes.

A few months before, I had been in a French town of the same kind, and Kutná Hora was lifeless by comparison; it was placid. Up in the cathedral gardens, mothers sat sewing beside their perambulators; old men sat under the limes; a college girl posed romantically on a rock under a tree, writing in her exercise book. A group of sixty or seventy lively teen-agers were taken round the church, which is full of beautiful things. The head boy translated the guide's comments into German for me. They were a gay lot of young people dressed like their kind anywhere in the West, and all Catholics—the boy said—for Czecho-slovakia is a predominantly Catholic country. While I was looking over the garden wall of the fine, once-Jesuit seminary close to the cathedral, I spotted a tavern with a garden down in the ravine. It was hot. I was thirsty. I climbed down and drank a couple of the pleasantest glasses of beer of my life under a chestnut tree, listening to the postman getting drunk with some rural cronies. (The Czechs are not as serious and stolid as they often sound.) At the height of a war story he was telling, which I couldn't quite understand, except that it was about the Nazis, he fell off his bench into the yard, and the ducks and chickens rushed off in a cloud of dust. It was a slow, warm, lazy hour, and the stream jingled under the woods.

By the evening the little town went dead again. There was a historical film and an Italian film on at the cinema; one or two motor bicycles roared through; at ten, a lorry set down a couple of very fat, trousered women from the factory. The only other people about were a few waiting for the last bus and they were being entertained by the town drunk, a housepainter who, having daubed himself with paint, reeled about scaring the girls and making speeches about Communism and Capitalism. His antics caused embarrassed sniggers.

There are places of far greater interest than Kutná Hora in Bohemia, Moravia, and Slovakia. Almost due south of the town in the mountains close to the Austrian border there is, for example, the exquisite town of Telo, where the deeply arcaded streets and the beautiful Baroque façades take the breath of the connoisseur. In palaces, man-sions, castles, in mural paintings and carvings, the country is rich, indeed one of the richest in Europe. In Slovakia, the wilder landscape and the old peasant life give a romantic accent to the scene. The conflict between the aristocratic culture of "foreign" Austria and the native Czech has been, in the course of history, fructifying, and the state carefully preserves all beautiful things.

Throughout my stay in Czechoslovakia, Jaroslav Hašek's *The Good Soldier Schweik* was often in my mind. Schweik, a fictional private in the Czech army in the First World War and a shirker who posed as an idiot to annoy his Austrian officers, is known all over the world. His character raises a fundamental question. I discussed Schweik with all kinds of people and made a point of dining at U Kalicha, the modest eatinghouse in Prague where working-men go, and where Hašek used to dine every day. On the walls are cartoons illustrating scenes from the famous comedy; also, the celebrated, original, faded, fly-blown picture of the Emperor Franz Joseph still hangs there.

It was in this restaurant that a Schweik-ish scene took place. Unable to understand the Czech menu, I made animal noises—a cock crowing, a pig grunting, a cow mooing—to determine the meat dishes. Soon everyone joined in with talented imitations. When we became serious, a man said to me sadly, nodding at Schweik's picture: "We Czechs have lost the art of laughing at ourselves." Schweik is respected as a historical object by middle-aged members of the Party, but they say he has nothing in common with the Czech today because "the situation has changed." The one or two young writers I spoke to did not think so.

Schweik is old-fashioned, they argued, but he still represents the traditional Czech device of malingering under a tyranny.

The traveller will remember the anxious, difficult smile of his Czech friends and will reflect that they are the people of a country only forty-two years old, living at the heart of the tangle of Central European history, and that under their domestic calm they accept the strain of it. But whether it is true that, given a chance, 90 per cent of the population would throw the Party out, no one can tell. One can only say that "rising" and "throwing out" are foreign to their cautious tempers.

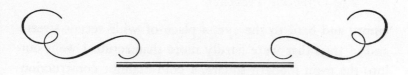

POLAND

At the end of the late September afternoon, the bed of cloud suds over which we had been flying from Frankfurt onwards, broke at last. Startling chasms, thousands of feet deep, opened; bands of green and blue sky appeared at strange angles, and on the floor of each canyon we caught sight of little strips of the Polish steppe. Villages looked grey, the land more unkempt than anything we had looked down on since Brussels or London, as we came down below the cloud. The airport building in Warsaw was stark and small. We got into an old bus and drove down dusty roads under yellowing trees and past miles of beetroot and cabbage gardens. There was ice in the grey evening air.

The first, false impression was of a new stone city,

41

empty and hard to the eye, a place of wide recent streets and of trees that were hardly more than scrub. I went out into the main modern square, a cold Stalinist construction of windy arcades, to a rendezvous with a young journalist. Just as he arrived on his scooter I heard laughter. Two middle-aged men were playing hide-and-seek with each other in the arcades, popping their heads out and calling "Bo!" to each other. At last, exhausted, they stopped, said a few parting words, kissed each other on the lips, and went off. My young friend glanced at them as I got on the back of his scooter.

"Everyone in Poland is mad," he shouted over his shoulder as we shot off across the city. "Anything can happen here. Anything can be said. You can do anything that comes into your head."

At my ears, as we whizzed along in the dark, there was not only the cold night wind, but the gusts of careless talk, high spirits, and folly. The young man was a Party member, in trouble with everyone. Of all the satellite countries, Poland is the largest, the poorest, the most terribly devastated by war, the most difficult in prospect, and by far the most vital and exciting. Whatever may depress or alarm the Western visitor—and the poverty is depressing—he will be astounded by the vivacity and independence of the people. They quarrel in the streets, they say what they like, they work and they laugh.

"The whole city was rebuilt from nothing in a few years! By the people themselves," my young friend shouted as we swayed and whizzed across the city. Volunteer workers were still loading rubble onto trucks in the bomb sites: there was not a street without scaffolding. The raw rough red brick had yet to get its coat of plaster on scores of buildings, but the beautiful old part of the city which the Nazis had taken a special pleasure in burning has been rebuilt in precise facsimile. They put it all back brick by brick, and when they ran short of the genuine brick they had the old brick copied. When there were no plans to go by, they drew on the paintings of Canaletto, whose pictures had luckily been bought by Polish landowners in the eighteenth century.

"Ninety per cent of the industrial buildings, eighty-five per cent of the houses, were destroyed," shouted my young friend. Six hundred thousand civilians died in Warsaw during the war. Six million people were murdered in Poland—and I mean murdered, for military losses were relatively small—four million, a very large number of them Jews, died in Auschwitz. The horror of it never leaves one's mind. Every open space, every public garden, is haunted. Wherever one stands in Warsaw the dust blows out of the side streets and it is as if human dust were blowing into one's eyes.

Young men and girls were hanging about that night in the old city, playing accordions and guitars. There is always something going on in a Warsaw street at night. Polish tempers are high and the vodka flows. I rarely went out without seeing the beginnings of a street scuffle, with friends dropping their briefcases and pulling the opponents away from each other. There was also a certain dangerous quizzical pride about the young. When my young friend got off his scooter in the old square, two young dandies came up and challenged him with a nod of amused contempt: "Well! What's this?"

"What is what?"

"This," nodding to the scooter.

"French motor scooter," said my friend, and gave a nod telling them to buzz off.

"Oh," they said, examining the situation to see if it offered an opportunity for trouble. After long, leisurely, impertinent stares they dawdled off. They guessed he was a Party member and were taking it out of him. It was all a little like that man-to-man challenging that goes on in Spain, not quite dangerous but not quite safe either.

We went down into the cellar of a youth club, popularly known as "the madhouse." It had long, heavy oak tables in it and the walls painted in tachiste style.

"Not exactly Socialist Realism," I said.

"That's finished here. We do what we like. It shocks the Russians," said my young Communist. One might have been in any Western city among the bearded boys in windjackets or check shirts, the girls in tight black jeans. We drank red wine and talked. We talked for hours.

Conversation with Communists has, as a rule, painful limitations. It is like conversation with Seventh-Day Adventists. Either one is dealing with people who smile obsequiously on one side of their faces and are like stone on the other, or one is trying to stop them from delivering the monologue one already knows by heart. Eastern European Communists are naturally more various than the Communists of Great Britain and the United States. They have to live Communism and adapt themselves to its changes.

44

Communism looks fixed to us; for them it is always in
flux. There is, for example, a great difference of mind between old, middle-aged, and young; the young Communists are bothered, curious, and flexible. On this first evening in Warsaw—and all my stay in Poland confirmed it—I
saw that Polish patriotism is far more important than
Communist doctrine to the Poles; and that to speak fearlessly, freely, exactly what comes into their heads, is the
Polish nature. For two hundred years the Poles have had
the habit of rebellion against authority. They find the
Russians admirable in many ways, but dull. No Pole can
resist the love story of Lara in *Dr. Zhivago*. They say they
did not publish *Dr. Zhivago* in order not to offend the
Russians. (However, they are not as delicate as all that.
They are not allowed to publish Evelyn Waugh's *Scott
King's Modern Europe*.) They are maliciously delighted
because the brilliant Polish magazine *Polska*—by far the
cleverest and most originally produced propaganda magazine in Eastern Europe—has had to be especially censored
in its Russian edition. The Russians—as a Salinger hero
would say—"kill" them. Polish culture, they insist, is
Western to the core. Hungarians say the same—but with
discreet periphrasis. Freedom is the fundamental Polish
passion: the freedom they lack is the freedom to print
entirely what they talk. This worried my young friend
the journalist; he accepted the Party line—"but I will
never write anything against my conscience. If I lived in
the West I'd probably be simply a Left-Wing Socialist."
My middle-aged Polish friends were worried about him,
but they were very tolerant. He belonged, they said, to

45

what is called the "mad faction." And the thirty-year-olds of the "mad faction" are in turn very critical of the generation who grew up after the war, who did not know the fight against the Nazis or the terror. My young friend said they were irresponsible, jazz-mad, Elvis Presley fans, and "car hungry." Politics and social questions bore them. Worse—they don't want to be engineers, unless they are of working-class origins, and Poland needs engineers. My young man was the last of the puritans. He was twenty-nine. There must be many of his kind who had been platoon leaders in the street fighting at the age of sixteen in the Siege, with boys of eleven under him. (One group of these children held a street for seventeen days against the Nazis.) He himself was the son of a self-educated factory worker, an old Communist, who was killed in a street battle against the Germans. The son admired his father enormously and quoted his sayings. He was proud that his mother, although a peasant woman, was a "noble," for many peasant families had a "noble" as distinct from a serf past. He had gone to the university—a rare experience for a worker's son in his father's generation.

I went later on to his flat up a leafy avenue out of the centre of the city. The flat was in one of the standard six-storey apartment blocks, plain, but agreeable in style, with poplars and maples planted around it and the grass getting worn by children. There was a stone staircase; also a lift. Like all young men of his age, my friend rushed in and put the gramophone on and then went for his wife, a shy, neat, pretty girl wearing a vermilion dress. She had the lovely fair hair and blue eyes of so many of the girls in

Warsaw—if the sun strikes a street full of them when they come out of their offices at half past three, one has the impression of seeing a cloud of dancing haloes. She was his second wife. He had divorced his first wife eighteen months ago, he said, "for political reasons," and there had been earlier troubles: she was Jewish and his parents had opposed the marriage.

The young couple's flat had three smallish rooms, one of which, under the room-rationing system, they were obliged to sublet. The Poznań rising in 1956—like the rising in Hungary—was due a good deal to anger at the housing situation and not entirely to low wages and resentment at the presence of Russian troops. My friends were lucky to have their place. The sitting room had hundreds of books in it; a lot of them were political—there were a good number of English and American books. Pointing to the collected works of Stalin, he told me he had downgraded them to a lower shelf. "You see," he said, "I move with the times." Puritans are adept at the comedies of conscience. On the wall was one of the tachiste paintings that he liked and, sure enough, there were Kafka's novels on the shelf—for Kafka is admired in Poland. *The Trial* and *The Castle* are on sale in all the street bookstalls of Warsaw. This taste shocks Western Communists and Left-Wingers generally, who, with the ingrained insensibility of the political mind, had regarded Kafka as a decadent, bourgeois abomination. To my friend, and all his circle, Kafka is the one writer who describes the conflicts in the Eastern European's mind and especially the Party member's! We sat up late eating bortsch, veal and rice and onions and drinking that peculiar vodka which is given a flavour a little like vanilla by a blade of grass that stands in the bottle.

At eleven o'clock the streets were empty, except for one or two drunks in the main square. There are one or two dull night clubs and there was an excellent satirical cabaret run by the students in a small builder's hut in the ruins. There is dancing to very old-fashioned tunes in the two main hotels. Except for these pockets of gaiety, the Warsaw nights are silent. The characteristic sound is the plop, plop, plop of a horse cab or, more often, of a cart carrying a load of bricks. One looks out of the window and sees that some enterprising man has been collecting bricks for himself from a bomb site; he is probably going to build a one-room house, a kind of box, on a patch of land among the trees on the outskirts of the city on the far side of the Vistula. This is against the law, but the authorities cannot do much about it. Sometimes they fine the builder, who gladly pays. He may even be fined once a year. He shrugs his shoulders; the fine is the rent as far as he is concerned. His house will be a simple box of one room with a door and a large window to it. In a year or two he will add another box. Later, if he can get hold of some plaster or cement, he will cover the brick, if his enthusiasm has not died. Polish enthusiasms do die. Outside Warsaw hundreds, indeed thousands, of these box houses dot the plain. They are the sign of a man who has begun life from the bare surface of the earth with what tools he could lay hands on. One of the young waiters at my hotel told me a bit of the story of his life which must be typical of the lives of many an ordinary man.

"I came back to Poland from France at the end of the war," he said. "In France the Germans had put me to work in the mines at Valenciennes. I was sixteen and was glad to be back because Poles are despised in France and in many foreign countries. 'Drunk as a Pole,' people say. We have a bad reputation. I never regretted returning. My wages are lower than a factory worker's, but I make something on tips. I've got a motorbike and now I'm married. My father-in-law built himself a room out in the fields and how he lived in that first year is a miracle. Luckily he was a carpenter and a mason. He had nothing but the clothes he stood in. It took him six months to find his wife and children. Now he has added another little room. My wife and I and our daughter live in that one. And," he added with dignity, *"it has its own door."*

The only complaint he had—and he whispered it— was that you did not know what was going to happen from day to day. "Now we are freer than we used to be; tomorrow it may come to an end." The State changes its plans. Things go wrong, are altered, new drives and policies start up and peter out.

"The great mistake you Westerners make about us," another Polish acquaintance said, "is that you think we are enslaved by a rigidly organized system from which one cannot escape. But the truth is that there is no real system. There is a state of continual disorder. Planners make small miscalculations which lead to enormous mistakes. And the ordinary man spends a lot of his time picking his way through chaos. For example, the population grows fast, people stream into the cities; then the planners discover that food is short and that we have to have queues at the butchers' and have one meatless day a week."

One does not hear people speaking as plainly as this in Czechoslovakia or Romania.

Warsaw is poor in restaurants. The two or three large hotels are fairly modern and good, but they are packed out with travellers attending conferences. Large parties of foreigners, fifty or a hundred at a time, come in from the Communist countries. I saw them sitting patient and drab in the restaurant, among the foreign traders and speculators, waiting to be served by half-trained waiters who were quarrelling with the manager. It often took me as much as two hours to get a simple meal. If customers complain the manager runs off in a panic. At one hotel I saw four waiters, who had decided not to attend to the customers, sitting on either side of the wide passage that led to the kitchen. Their stretched-out legs nearly met in the middle. They were waiting to trip up the manager when he came by; he had to hop over them as best he could. There is a peculiar, sharp backwards gesture of the open hand which Poles use to express angry contempt. The waiters used it often and then, to recover their calm, went off to have a pull at some customer's carafe of vodka on the serving table. The lack of discipline becomes eventually as enjoyable as an Irish farce. But any Pole who comes back from Russia is delighted to remark that the chaos is far worse there. "Go out of Moscow to some provincial town," they say. "You'll soon see." But so long as the Pole has his café and his cup of strong black coffee, a place where he can sit because he may be living in an overcrowded flat, he does not complain. There are one or two amusing café bars where waiters and artists meet and concoct the jokes about Communism which circulate throughout Eastern Europe.

To travel is to live in an extreme state of mind, the eyes and ears alerted; but one pays for it in spells of loneliness, boredom, and personal melancholia. The mind has worked too hard and one is left in a condition of resentful loneliness. There was an elderly Belgian business-man in a bar who had been coming to Poland all his life and who did tricks with matchboxes.

"Ah well," he sighed when he packed up. "It passes the time. It provides a little comedy." And the twinkling old self-therapist waddled off to bed. I must say I had less of this boredom in Warsaw than I have had in other countries.

The book shops in Warsaw are good. One can buy Western papers; one can read in the many public reading rooms a great many Western reviews. The cultural attach-ment to the West is too strong to be broken. The theatre produces the best new European playwrights and does not stick only to Shaw, Shakespeare, and *Look Back in Anger*. I saw a delightful play, *Parady* by Jan Potocki—a witty late-eighteenth-century charade with a lineage running from *The Beggar's Opera* to vaudeville and pantomime—and the audience laughed loudly when one of the actors mimicked Gomulka's tub-thumping style of oratory. (Gomulka, a real solid peasant, shrewd, obstinate, un-pretentious, is regarded with affection and admiration; they pray that he will not be paralyzed by Party intrigue.) I was astounded to find a delightful production of Thornton

Wilder's *The Matchmaker*. There is a shortage of cinemas, and one has to book days ahead to get a seat in them, but I managed to get into *The Train*. Jaded by the clichés of Hollywood, one is excited and refreshed by the Polish cinema. It has never occurred to the Poles to fake; they have emancipated themselves from propaganda and in their nationalism they approach the Italians. The Polish film makers are fortunate. They can get all the money they need and do not have as much trouble with the censorship as writers do. "We are beginning to wonder," an editor said to me, "if general poverty such as we have here is not a great advantage to the arts. The public taste is not corrupted by materialism." But the writers do not find life very easy. The Party has been through a phase of indulgence, hoping that greater liberty would entice the writers out of silence or mediocrity. The editor told me that this had not succeeded. The writers are in a state of mistrust. They argue that in Poland things can change overnight. They improve and then worsen with the whims of policy—since I was in Warsaw they have tightened up again. Above all, the writers have come to mistrust themselves. It is not only a question of "Shall I be allowed to say this or that?" but "Ought I to or am I sure?" It must be remembered that on the continent of Europe and especially in Poland writers have traditionally had great public prestige and are thought of in Shelleyan terms, as the legislators. There are far too many painters, and the State has a great stock of pictures on its hands that it does not know what to do with. There are no private buyers. Something is done to divert the painters to applied art; and, in fact, some of the best Polish artists have turned out some fine posters.

I was never bored by Polish conversation: it has some
affinities with Irish talk. I was never bored by the streets.
The Poles go to work early and finish at three-thirty in the
afternoon. Then comes the rush hour of golden-headed
girls and men with briefcases. They rush for the trams and
hang on anywhere. Those dense clusters of human beings
hanging on the trams are called "the grapes." Later on, in
the evening, one sees many of this crowd returning to some
extra job which city people have to do to support themselves. It is usual for both husband and wife to work in
order to get enough to live on. Over the river in Praga is
the poor quarter, overcrowded and lively, where a family
of seven will often be found living in one room. This
quarter has a free market which my friends were ashamed
of: although not Party members, they thought there was
something disgraceful and dishonest about private trade
like this. They regarded a free market as a swindle and said
a lot of the stuff was stolen or smuggled. The market in
Praga is a collection of tiny booths selling old clothes, displays of gaudy oleographs, stockings, boots. There was a
very fine and pretty show of bridal dresses. There was an
old lady, a herbalist and witch, I suppose, who wore two
pairs of glasses, one of them dark blue—the wearing of
blue glasses was an affectation of the Russian nihilists in the
nineteenth century; perhaps hers had somehow come down
to her from them! She was selling what looked like big
knobs of rock or fossil, but which turned out to be the
parasitic whorls of wood that grow on the trunks of trees.
She told us they were a well-known cure for cancer and
showed us a newspaper cutting in which an American
doctor said there was something in the notion. She could

recite the medical jargon. There was an old man who was carrying strings of dried mushrooms over his shoulder like beads. "Gomulka doesn't approve of this place," my friends persisted. But the crowd liked it. The sellers rushed out with skirts, dresses, and coats on their arms into the crowd, shouting. The State had its own small hut there too, selling slippers at clearly marked prices. No one was at the State stall. People preferred to haggle.

"Selling things on the arm" is one of the lowest occupations. It causes shame to families. I had one Polish acquaintance who had an aunt who did this. "I regard my family," he said, "as a cross section of the new Poland. My father was a factory worker, killed by the Germans; my mother a simple peasant, devoutly Catholic. My first aunt was a beautiful peasant girl. She became a *cocotte*, lived with various rich men, married a fashionable hairdresser in Warsaw, and was murdered by the Nazis. My second aunt, a shopkeeper, is the most detestable conventional type of petit bourgeoise, who now pretends she has read all the latest books. My third aunt, the simple one, sells clothes on the arm in the markets and lives in misery. Myself—an atheist and a lecturer. My brother an engineer. We are the history of modern Poland."

Each one has his revolutionary story. There was and is no such thing as evasion and being noncommittal. There is the once enormously rich and powerful landowner Prince Radziwill living in his little Warsaw flat among a few of his treasures. The Prince was a leader of the Right-Wing Party before the war, bitterly anti-Communist, strictly Catholic, and a great landowner. He is a figure very much admired

54

for his aristocratic and disdainful handling of German gen-
erals during the war. He asked a group of them to dinner
and made them eat the starvation rations they allowed the
Poles, served with full ceremony. His country house outside Warsaw is now a national museum and writers go there
to work. The family servants still work there, and the old
gentleman anxiously enquires from time to time if "the
service is as good as it used to be." I think of a middle-
aged lawyer who had been sent by his family to London
when he was young to toughen up by working in the dock
quarter. He grew up to manage the legal affairs of a great
Polish estate and became a small landowner himself. When
the State took over his land, his peasants came to him and
gave him all the rents they had saved up during the Nazi
occupation. He was a man of great charm who liked good
food and was finicky about good tailoring. "There is no
excuse for a man being poorly dressed in Warsaw," he said.
"It is a city of tailors, and if anyone tells you a cadging
story about needing new clothes, you can be sure he is a
fool living beyond his means." Or I think of that tragic
road on the far side of the Vistula where hundreds of thousands of civilians marched out in 1940 to join regiments
which had already been overrun and scattered and were to
fall in the great common graves that were discovered
towards the end of the war. It was down this road, in a chic
garden café for polite Sunday excursions, that a worried
middle-aged official told me of the trouble he had with his
young daughter. "She hates politics, she sneers at the
Party"—his party—"she won't work. When I ask 'What is
the matter with you and your generation?' she says 'We

55

are bored, bored. We want a good time.' 'Do something,' I say. 'There is nothing to do,' she says, and sulks. Is it the same in the West? I can't get anything out of her." I think of the professor laughing: "How can *they* know how many pickled cucumbers everyone is going to eat during the next three years; and if they don't, how can they correctly plan the number of glass jars they will require for them?"

Except for the skyscraping Palace of Culture, which dominates the city like some absurd wedding cake—it was a Russian present to the Poles, who mock and shudder at its vulgarity—Warsaw is a low-built place and the sky is wide and seems to come down to the streets. The clouds of pigeons, whose wings darken and then are as dazzling as bits of tinfoil as they turn in the sky, seem to go higher than any other birds I have seen wheeling over cities. Outside Warsaw, on the Polish Plain, the sky seems to come down to one's feet and one feels that only a few chance trees prevent one from seeing for hundreds of miles all the way to Berlin in the west and to Moscow in the east. It is not a monotonous plain, for it is made gentle, graceful, and a little melancholy by poplars and willows, by little woods and dark bands of forest. The famous empty paved road to Poznań and Berlin lies under oaks and ashes that are all movement, and in the autumn when I was driving down it, the poplars were already turning yellow and the maples were reddening.

One drives through the outlying suburbs of Warsaw, half shattered, half rebuilt, and across fields and fields of huge cabbages, and the road cuts into the plain as straight as a knife. It is close-cobbled and sometimes macadamized and very good, but the side roads are dusty and rough, for the soil of the Vistula basin is sandy. (The wide river has never been made navigable: the Poles give a temperamental sigh of self-criticism when they recall that the Germans made all the German rivers navigable a hundred years ago. This is, once more, the kind of conversation one has in Ireland, and the smell of turf smoke circling out of cottage chimneys increases one's Irish sensations. But the Irish have no coal and the Poles have too much: in the present coal slump they are dumping it unwanted in the countryside.)

People often say that the Polish Plain is even more monotonous than the prairie of Canada. This complaint arises from the excessive admiration given to mountain scenery since the Romantic movement and also from the special boredom that long train journeys introduced to the human mind. Like all great plains, Poland's has the freedom and illumination of a vaster sky than we usually see; the variety and play of light are delicate. The long sky stands over the long distances and brings something changeable, tender, lonely, and lyrical to the scene. The poplars and willows, the small woods and the bands of forest, give it the grace of continual and quiet disclosure. Chopin's house—where they now give informal concerts—is in this country, and one cannot resist the feeling that the lyricism and the sharply changing moods of his music owe something to the landscape. Nostalgia is natural to places where light and distance are so long. Cornflowers and scabious were growing in the ditches, and the road runs under the shade of the oak, the ash, and the poplar. It was a Sunday when I drove along it, and we occasionally saw youths out partridge shooting. They wore the curiously military dress of the people: stiff, black peaked caps and high black boots.

The villages have the Irish negligence. The cottages were single-storey buildings, thatched with rushes. The small windows were filled with geraniums and other window plants and were hung with lace curtains. The cottages usually have two rooms—a summer room and a winter room, the latter with a bulky tiled stove in one corner reaching to within a couple of feet of the ceiling. In another corner is a single bed piled with quilts. At night those members of the family who cannot squeeze into the bed sleep on the floor and the young children are put on top of the stove.

It was the church-going hour and soon we picked up files of peasants who were walking miles to church at the fast Sunday stride. In this part of the country they are droll, starling figures—the huge men in the orange-and-black-striped pantaloons worn under a long black overcoat flowing out over their high black boots, and the women, immensely petticoated under their bunched-out skirts, which are hidden by a black apron in front and have broad stripes of gaudy green, yellow, violet, and red at the back. The bodies are black. The women's skirts are worn in pairs and are weighted with sequins, so that they are heavy to wear; but peasant women are strong. They march like men. It is a marvel that the girls can dance in this costume, but once they are worked up to the full spin of the mazurka, they can make these weighty skirts whirl like a spinning top.

We went into two churches that Sunday, the huge, ugly,

glazed pink-brick church of a tiny hamlet, and afterwards into the splendid church, in the Baroque style, of the town of Lowicz. The sense of theatre is strong in the Polish people. They love gaudy colours. Inside the village church, the sight was startling. A dozen heavy ropes or festoons made of green moss were looped from the high roof to within a yard of our heads, and among them hung gaudily painted emblems, shields, and medallions belonging to the brotherhoods of the church. Between them hung elaborate mobiles of tinsel and cut-out paper which are traditional in the folk art of the Poles; I've seen dozens of these exquisite and brilliant fantasies in many Polish cottages and museums. The walls were garishly painted. It was like being inside some childish fair booth or box of toys. The place was icy cold, and at first we thought it empty. Then we noticed that two or three old women, wrapped in grey and black blankets, were sitting in the pews. Suddenly one of them struck up a raucous chanting; the chant was taken up by one or two of the others, and these harsh and eerie high-pitched sounds came echoing off the walls more like the beating of buckets and pails than the sound of the human voice.

In Lowicz the performance was less primitive; indeed we were present at the Mass. The church is a fine piece of Baroque, with rearing statues and soaring angels, and in this theatrical setting, the country people stood or knelt. One woman, a penitent, in the full finery of the country, knelt barefooted at the head of the crowd before the altar, which had grouped itself instinctively as if it were a crowd in a play. Once again when the choir sang we heard that harsh, shrill, hoarse note of Polish religious song, though here it had the purity of training. The country people looked as if they had been carved out of wood; and out of the wood stared the large, carven, steady blue eyes that seem to be the mark of the Slav. Afterwards we went to a smoky restaurant in the town, to eat a watery stew of tripe with fennel floating in it, and then potato salad and ham; every time we finished our large glasses of vodka, the solid wench in her white apron rushed to bring us another. The glass must never be empty. The place filled up with young men and women from cyclists' clubs and the weekend motorcyclists, for all the countryside had come in to Lowicz to eat, drink, and hang about the square, thousands of them in their best clothes. There were buses and even half a dozen motorcars. The vodka got us talking, and naturally we were talking about politics, about the peasants, the land, and the Catholic Church. My friends were not Communists but they were strong supporters of Gomulka.

For Gomulka, a peasant himself, had allowed the dissolution of the State farms and co-operatives, which had been the heart and soul of Communist agriculture up to 1956. Out of 10,000 large State farms, there are only 2,000 left. The Polish peasant has always fanatically wanted his few poor acres for himself and nobody else. He has lived badly on uneconomic patches for centuries; the population is growing at a terrible speed and he lives worse. "Yet," my friends kept saying, "they have shoes. They are well clothed. We have at any rate seen to that." Once he had got his way, the peasant grew more, worked harder, may even have looked after the machinery properly instead of leav-

ing it to fall to pieces. The bigger farmers, the so-called
kulaks, who had been expropriated, were not permitted to
come back—many of them had in fact taken the chance
to become small farmers—but slowly (I was told) some of
the peasants have seen advantages in co-operation and are
joining once more. They malingered when forced; self-
interest has led some back to voluntary associations, and
this is what the Party hopes for.

The Roman Catholic Church is as powerful in Poland as
it is in Ireland. No government can dispense with it, ignore
it, or completely override it in this peasant country. Under
Gomulka, it has become the great negative force. It is not
persecuted—there are no political prisoners in Poland—
and the Archbishop's sermons on political co-operation in
Warsaw every Sunday morning are famous and crowded.
All the same, there are often serious clashes between priests
and commissars. The State may set up its birth-control
clinics; the Church does not protest, but it sees to it that
propaganda is not distributed and that the clinics do not
thrive. And (again, like the Irish peasant) the Polish peasant
is puritanical and severe in the matter of sexual knowledge
and morality. It seems that Polish women marry earlier and
have more children than they did before the war. The land
is crowded; the big cities are crowded, because there has
been a rapid advance towards industrialism; only the small
market towns are getting smaller. This is partly due to the
extermination of tens of thousands of Jewish shopkeepers
under the Nazis, and to the nationalization of the retail
trade.

Because we can talk freely to the Poles we must be

careful not to misunderstand them. They enjoy calling themselves the "mad Poles" just as the Irish enjoy calling themselves the "mad Irish." They have had two hundred years as an enslaved nation, and they have the tradition of being "agin the government." But just as the Irish no longer hate the British, so the Poles no longer hate the Russians; indeed they are bound to Russia by the common historic dread of German invasion. Even in the matter of the Russian halt at the siege of Warsaw—a theme over-exploited by American propaganda—they are far from being totally critical of the Russians. The Poles see themselves as the one real intermediary between the East and West, for their religion and culture are Western. "We are the French of Eastern Europe." And like all the Central European satellites, they regard the withdrawal of British political influence in the thirties with bitterness; just as they regard American anti-Communism as hysterical and ill-informed and the American support of West Germany as dangerous. On the long straight road from Berlin to Warsaw, across that defenceless plain, the Polish attitude is vividly understandable.

HUNGARY

Y ou're lucky," said the French-speaking lady in Bratislava, where the Danube bends on the border of Czechoslovakia and Hungary. I had told her I was off to Budapest, less than an hour away by plane. She was a Slovak who hated speaking German, so we used to have rather formal and histrionic conversations in our best French. "Ah, Budapest!" she said. "The Hungarian women are so pretty and they have wonderful taste in clothes and you'll eat well there. They're gay and lighthearted. Not like us."

"Even after the Rising?" I asked.

"Yes," she said. "They forget quickly. Things are better there. You will have friends everywhere."

She was right.

The flight from Bratislava to Budapest is short. One is

immediately struck by the change of scene from the thickly wooded, mountainy land of Czechoslovakia. One is flying over the wide Danube Valley and over low hills towards the Hungarian Plain. It is as flat as a table and occupies a very large part of the country. One is flying also into a softer, if erratic, climate, where the sun is kind, the cattle graze, and the vine grows well—a wine-drinking land. Yellow and grey, bristling in the sun, dotted with small agricultural towns and red-roofed villages that do not huddle, but spread out into little draught boards of red boxes, the plain is rich. Before American and Canadian wheat came on the market in the nineteenth century, this plain supplied large areas of Europe. It is not a land of poor, ignorant peasants; every traveller is struck by the high material and cultural level of the countryman's life in the little market towns. The Danube comes through it lazily on its way south to Yugoslavia, and it is surprising to hear that, in this mild climate, the river freezes up in the short winter when the east wind blows. Hungary is a small country—it has dwindled seriously since the two world wars and is only 122 miles long and 280 miles wide, with a population of just under ten million. The Hungarians often speak of "going to the mountains" for their holidays, and certainly there are mountains to the northeast and southwest of Budapest, but they are not mountains as their neighbours in Austria, Yugoslavia, and Czechoslovakia know them.

The French lady was right. Except about the forgetting. The sun dazzled, the autumn air was warm and sleepy at the handsome airport in Budapest. The officials had the negligence and excitability of lazy men in uniform. One saw a few Gypsyish faces outside, and when the dusty old taxi broke down as it took me by the *Autobahn* into the city, I laughed with pleasure. We were certainly outside efficient, Germanic Europe. We broke down again in a mile-long traffic jam of lorries and horses and carts. Everyone was grinning, shrugging, or shouting. One might have been in Italy or Spain. It was one of the most cheerful traffic jams I have ever been in. They often occur in Hungary because, during the Rising, the Russian tanks made a mess of the roads.

Happiness continued. I stayed on the Margaret Island, that long island of beautiful trees, winding paths, and formal gardens, tennis clubs, boating clubs, and hot springs where the happy rheumatics sit in the volcanic water in the open-air baths, simmering quietly like pork in the sun. There are 123 thermal springs in Budapest, and thousands of people take the waters every day. In the hotel gardens one dined or drank at the basket tables under the trees, and at night there was dancing under the stars to old-fashioned tunes. The people appeared to be comfortable middle-aged persons living on their means: not entirely a delusion. There were no Americans, which was startling. The American government did not allow its citizens to visit Hungary; I do not know if this is still so. In the open-air cafés the orchestras played. The flowers—especially the red canna —were sumptuously spread. Pretty girls brought the beer, the wine, or the Hungarian salami. Wandering about the shady paths in the heat of the morning, one saw chattering troops of children from the creches or kindergartens following their nurses. Hoses twirled their spray over the lawns. The gardeners were flirting with the stout young peasant girls, whose dark hair was done in bright handkerchiefs and who were pretending to sweep the paths. Everyone has an obligation to work, and one of the lasting impressions of the People's Democracies is that they are places where women of all ages have the agreeable job of gossiping with friends as they lean on their brooms before sweeping an almost invisible heap of dust a few feet from one part of the paths to another and then leaning contentedly on the brooms again.

Up and down the river went the white paddle steamers and pleasure launches. Late in the afternoon the rowing eights and diamonds were sparkling like water flies, the women's crews as strenuous as the men's; and all the seats under the trees by the river were occupied by pairs of lovers. There seemed to be a special technique for courtship on the Margaret Island which I have never seen elsewhere: the girl sits on the seat, the man sitting beside her puts his legs through the back of the seat, so that he can face her. So, with his back to the passers-by, the uninhibited Hungarian shuts out the world and concentrates on the beautiful thing and avoids the spine and waist twisting of the ordinary sideways embrace. In the meantime, the crews cried from the river, the tennis balls slapped onto the courts, the footballers and basketball players shouted in the distance; then the lights came on among the trees, the Hungarian owls began making their curious yelping noise in the branches as if they were flying dogs; the Red Star shone on the tower of the enormous Gothic Parliament

House, and the lights prickled over the steep hills of Buda and in the flat city of Pest. The buses arrived, bringing the crowds to the open-air theatre.

I went there that night with a clever young man who was an authority on William Blake and who had just edited a selection of his works. The translation and interpretation of *Visions of the Daughters of Albion* had caused him a lot of worry, but Hungarians have considerable reason for thinking themselves the best translators in the world. They produce Shakespearean scholars by the dozen and think that Hungarian translations of the poet surpass the German. We sat in the warm September air under the stars in this pleasant modern theatre. We were seeing a traditional operetta of the old-fashioned kind: *János Vitéz* by Kacsóh. It has pretty tunes and all the things that Hungarians love—the scenes of peasant life, the shepherd with his flock that wanders in from the real trees, a gallop of splendid Hussars, a victory over the Turks, and a splendid court scene on the Versailles model where the decadent Prince confronts the stalwart hero and the court ladies perform a ballet. "Simple people," my friend said, nodding to the audience. It was a popular show.

The wide coppery-green Danube sweeps in a long curve under the eight bridges which have been rebuilt since the war and divides Buda from Pest. It is a city of some 1,700,-000 people. Thousands crowd the trolley buses and suburban trains. On the Pest side, the Hungarian Plain begins at once. Pest is flat, and here are the fashionable streets, the once famous restaurants and cafés. They survive. Budapest thought of itself as another Paris—so did Bucharest in Romania—and still tries to think so. The shops in the fashion-able streets do their best to keep up an air of the *ancien régime*. People dress well. The dress shops, the hat shops, the tailors and shirtmakers, put up a show. Hungarians dress for the street. Now and then one sees an elderly couple go by who might even be called fashionable. How they con-trived to be so was a mystery to me; but I was told that they might be people with top jobs in State Industry, or they might have had a big house in the past or valuable pictures and so on, which they could sell. Or they might be living on some pension, although the pensions of the middle classes were slashed to very little. Old age generally means work in Hungary, not retirement. But if private savings were confiscated, things were not. I did not see any severe poverty in Hungary, and although the country became much smaller after the First World War, and smaller still after the Second, it was a well-found little nation and was already getting on its feet industrially before the war. One of the complaints against the Russians at the time of the Ris-ing in 1956 was that they had forced deliveries of Hun-garian goods into Russia at very unfavorable rates of exchange. Any Hungarian will tell you with pride that the *écrevisses* you ate in Paris probably came from Lake Balaton and that you certainly ate Hungarian chicken in Vienna; and that if Hungary has lost some of its Western markets, it has found new ones—Nasser's Egypt buys Hungarian trol-ley buses and motor lorries.

The walls of the shops and offices in Pest were still pocked with the bullets and shells of the Russian tanks in 1956, but new buildings are going up quickly where the

68

bombardment had been most destructive. The damage of the Rising was tackled quickly in order to wipe out the signs of that disastrous comment on the true relations of the People's Democracies with their ruling minority and with Soviet Russia. Up in Buda at the high point of the Horthy Palace, the citadel, the cathedral and castle, the destruction caused by the battle for Budapest in the Second World War was being repaired much more slowly. I went up many times to look for little garden cafés where Gypsies turn up to play, and to stand in the lovers' gazebo, a superb lookout point for a general view of the city. The lovers go up there to scratch their initials inside the little temple-like structure and look down on the river, the ochre-coloured buildings, the Baroque towers, and the mixed, but on the whole handsome, parade of buildings on the river front. The city is one that interests the eye.

In Budapest one falls immediately among friends. Everybody knows everybody else—in the most casual crowds at a bus stop or in an office, people always add some personal detail that is handed on; everyone loves talking; and the smallest bit of news travels in no time across the city. I hailed a taxi in the street after I had been there only a week and the taxi driver knew all about me: he had heard it from another taxi driver, who had heard it from a fare. It is true that taxi drivers were used as police informers before 1956, and perhaps still are; but as this one tried, in a mixture of night-school English and fragmentary German, to tell me why he considered *Othello* the greatest of Shakespeare's plays, I was not worried. In two or three days I had more acquaintances than I knew what to do with; all clever, all fizzing with argument and almost caressing in kindness, subtle, serious, passionate, and cynical, masters of irony. Notoriously this is a nation with more writers and intellectuals to the square mile than any other on earth. Like the Viennese, they spend a lot of time in cafés in long discussions, which emerge in articles, in reviews, in the theatre, and in novels. They have one exceptional quality: they are pretty well the only intellectuals in the world who often turn out to be first-rate bankers and financiers and who have a sound capacity for large practical enterprises. They are masterly impresarios in their own country, in London, Paris, Hollywood, and New York, many of them Jews who always held high positions under the old aristocracy though rarely penetrating that caste. I was cornered one evening by a young university lecturer who had amused himself by putting on a play or two in Budapest; he complained to me that he had not been able, so far, to obtain the Hungarian rights of *My Fair Lady*, which he wanted to put on! He wanted to take a big jump up the ladder. I tactfully pointed out the enormous personal and financial difficulty and the complication of the enterprise. But the lecturer on French poetry, I realized, was not a naïve dreamer in the eyes of his friends.

"We cannot understand why there should be any difficulty," they said.

"It is very important to make a great deal of money," he said. Clearly they had no doubt about the soundness of his proposal or his capacities. Hungarian ability is a serious thing.

But there was a shadow on our friendship. All the Hungarians I met, except three or four who were staunch Party members and had important jobs under the Kádár regime, made me swear not to write of any of their political views or to identify them. If I had lunch with one of them he would certainly send messages to me by a friend the following day, reminding me of my promise. But they all said with some pride—the Communist, the ex-Communist, and the anti-Communist: "We have got over the Rising. Life is back to normal, and we are even much better off than we were before it all happened, except for the human tragedy."

I said: "What about the six people who were executed a few weeks back for their part in the Rising?"

The reply to this was that what they meant by normality was "back to normal on the surface," and was put by a diplomat in these words: "The police surveillance is relaxed as far as the majority of people are concerned. It now operates in a more concentrated, efficient, and specialized way in the circles it is watching. The terror is far more severe." He was right at the time, but latterly friends tell me that the regime has become milder. The fact is that the political temperature goes up and down; one lives in an imposed climate, sometimes benign and sometimes chilly. The severity is felt chiefly by Party members—for the Rising began as a quarrel among the Communists themselves, and all are haunted by some degree of guilt. What really shocked the Hungarians was the Russian soldier's ignorance of the common amenities of civilization.

I went with a middle-aged Party member to a football match on my first Saturday afternoon. He was a reliable

Party man, proud of his "little family"—his wife and two children, who were doing well at high school—mad about football. There must have been 80,000 people at the match, but the teams were poor. He was frank about it: "The Rising has cost us the loss of a great deal of talent of all kinds," he said. "We lost our best football players. Two of them are now playing for Real Madrid"—of all Fascist teams!

"Politics are a curse," I said carelessly. "They are the cause of the whole of modern misery."

"Everything," he said severely, correcting me in the firmest Marxist manner, "is political."

I think I can quote him without getting him into trouble. I imagine his position was strong, since he was still a Party man.

The dilemma of the Party as a whole is that it is in conflict with its own nationalist feelings, for, like the Poles, the Hungarians are nationalists before everything else; their mistrust of Russia is traditional and their cultural traditions are overwhelmingly Western. The wretched Party members are always warning each other: "Be careful. That is how it begins."

What is "it"? Sin, of course. It is all right for an organization to have contact with the West, but for the individual it is perilous to say to the Westerner: "Send me that engineering textbook. Tell me how I can find out about the music or painting of So-and-So, about the health service in Great Britain or municipal government in Birmingham." There was some talk, when I was in Budapest, of arranging an exchange visit between the mayor of a Hungarian town and the mayor of an English industrial city.

"We are waiting for approval," said the busy official in the Foreign Ministry, who has about three telephone calls a minute. And he nodded from his window across the Danube to that modern building on *pilotes* which is beginning to look a bit grubby, as functional architecture so quickly does, the Ministry of the Interior, the headquarters of the police. Months later I was asked to a party in London to meet the chief of Hungarian municipalities, so I gather the permit came through for someone. In Budapest, where large numbers of people have read George Orwell's *1984* and *Animal Farm* (although they are banned), the Ministry of the Interior is known as the Ministry of Love. I had no difficulty in seeing and talking to innumerable Hungarians, and they were interesting and outspoken, as I have said, but they were all aware of the dangers of "it," whether they were in favour of the government or against it.

I have only one more thing to say about Hungarian politics. It is important and difficult to express. It is this. The revolt was a spontaneous mass rising of the people—so spontaneous that it was almost incompetent, and surprised the people themselves—and its suppression was tragic. It is the feeling of tragedy that remains and, with it, among ordinary people outside politics, the desire for healing of wounds. For this reason, many Hungarians who had been on the side of the Rising said to me that they were out of sympathy with the attitudes of the Hungarian refugees abroad. There is some envy in this: claustrophobia is the chief illness in the satellite countries. Some thought they should have stayed and lived through the aftermath, as my friends had had to do. Others said they should return and "be Hungarians." Others said that, with the passing of time, the refugees had lost their relevance and knowledge, and that their minds were dangerously fixed traumatically on the rebellion, whereas the situation in Hungary had moved on. Others resented the hostile propaganda of the refugees as "unpatriotic." Still others, the loss of active and virile population. As the months and years go by, the refugees lose their value as witnesses. Now, it is natural that obedient Communists should say this, but many of the people who said this were anti-Communists. They feel deeply the loss to the country, and this is a measure of the strength of Hungarian nationalism. In a practical way, the existence of large colonies of refugees in Vienna and elsewhere in the West has made it much more difficult to get what all satellite peoples long for—visas for travel. To meet a refugee abroad is a considerable sin, to stay in his house almost a crime. The government's foreign espionage service reports back to Budapest every movement of the sinner, even the shops that are visited, the trains taken, the car rides. This insecurity preys on the minds of the non-political; it haunts the Communist Party leaders. The Rising for them was a Party quarrel; they are all guilty. This was in 1960. In 1963 an anti-Stalinist purge theoretically softened the regime.

To go back to that football match. So that the crowd could get its money's worth, there were two games. We were there from two till six. The crowd had bursts of temperament. A woman sitting behind me grabbed my hat and screamed when a player missed a shot, and then collapsed with blushes when everyone laughed at her. One player, in a fury with the referee's whistle, kicked the ball far out into the crowd and got a formal dressing down on the field. We had all bought lottery tickets, and between the games the winners came out. One man won a woman's bicycle, another a radio, and another a television set. It is very difficult to walk round an arena carrying a television set: he had to get the police to help. Showers of lottery tickets went up in the air like confetti. There are not very many private cars in Budapest, and 80,000 people had to fight their way onto the trains and buses afterwards. I was lucky to have a lift in an old car borrowed from a doctor—after successful writers, doctors are the highest-paid people in Hungary and are among the first to get cars and telephones. After the match, I went off alone to the flat of an elderly, lively American lady, the widow of a Hungarian, who rejects all attempts by her American and Swedish relations to get her out. "I should be bored in New York or Stockholm," she said. "And the music is better here."

There were a lot of people in her three-room flat in a new modern block in Pest. She had been able to buy it under a new mortgage scheme, and had raised the money by selling one or two family pictures. She had been obliged by the housing law to let one room and the use of the kitchen to a young married couple. This started her off on the doctor problem, on marriage, women, and divorce, and everyone joined in. The young couple had been married before. The girl had divorced her husband because he had been thrown out of the Party and had lost his job. The new husband had also had a disaster. He had married a woman doctor who made a larger income—much larger

75

income—than his as a teacher, and she had left him, taking with her the car and the telephone!

"It is terrible the way you young people are behaving nowadays," the Swedish-born lady said. "There is a shocking number of divorces."

It is because it was almost impossible to get a divorce before 1956. Husbands and wives who were destroying each other not only could not get divorced but also couldn't find other rooms or flats to go to, owing to the housing shortage. "They still can't," someone said.

"I know cases where couples have 'separated' and have had to bring their new partners to live in the same tiny flat and no one knew whose children were whose," said someone else.

There was a quiet, poorly dressed woman of about thirty-five, a clerk in some municipal office. She had divorced her husband after waiting years for the change in the law.

"To live in Budapest," she said, "both husband and wife must have jobs, because salaries are low, but if the marriage is a bad one and gets on their nerves, the news soon gets round, and there are dozens watching them to take their places if their work falls off or they make a mistake. You just can't afford, for your job's sake, to have a bad home life."

"We can hardly ever meet, or we're tired out when we do," said a young man, talking of his girl. "We both have to have two jobs."

"Yet," said the tough old American lady, "you've got to admit that women have a much better status, are much more highly regarded by their neighbours and friends in this society, if they do work."

They all agreed on that. There was a rosy-faced, white-haired, very stout, energetic woman, excitable, clever, and talkative, who was wearing a brilliant red dress. She was a Greek scholar, and when she left with us and we took a fast trolley bus which rolled and swayed us all as we drove into Buda, she was laughing about what she was going to cook for her family's supper. She not only taught in the university but supported and looked after her family and nursed her husband, who was crippled and whose health had been wrecked by years in concentration camps. She was the jolliest woman I met in Hungary and, as some said, "one of the old Communist idealists—not one of the time-servers of today." Where does one not hear nowadays, East or West, that the young generation are time-servers and operators?

Traditionally Budapest was the gay city. One very old gentleman told me that the gaiety of the old days had vanished. I found him living in a rather impressive suburban house among his books and pictures, sitting morosely at a handsome table covered with drawings and eating corn on the cob, a rather buttery dish for a very old gentleman. He was cursing old age eloquently, appeared several times to nod off, spoke to me in several languages, and talked about the universal Hungarian subject—Shakespeare. He saw himself as Lear and was enjoying the part as he peered at his circle of admirers. Age and eminence are treated with profound respect in this country.

Despite the old man's anger against time, I found pockets

77

of gaiety in Budapest. That very evening, up in the hills from which Buda looks like a field of stars fallen to earth, some of us went to eat delicious pork cooked on a skewer and to drink white wine at a small tavern. Two or three parties had brought accordions to their tables; everyone was drunk and singing; carnations were being thrown at the pretty girls, and there was general uproar. The music echoed off the suburban woods and hills.

And then, in other places, there were the Gypsy orchestras. We were sitting in the courtyard under the trees of a modest café in Buda, where a few couples were drinking the delicate white wine. Painters, Hollywood films, and smart restaurants generally romanticize the Gypsy. In Hungary, which is, above all others, the country of Gypsy music, the Gypsy is a respectable-looking man in a navy blue serge suit. Certainly he is swarthy and dark-haired; one notices also two main types: the plump, short kind with congested face who looks like a prosperous lawyer, and the lean, emaciated, thin-lipped kind who looks like the devil. The unsmiling face, the indifferent manner, the impassivity with which they receive praise or insult or endure scornful neglect, their concern only for money and their amused ironical refusal to thank if they get it, are the qualities which give them a frightening distinction. They know they are able to create feeling in their audience and to play with detached cruelty upon them until one is, for the moment, in their impudent and yet negligent power. There are bad Gypsy players in Budapest, but the good ones know how to fill slowly every molecule of the air with their smoky, sullen chords that rumble like fire shut

78

up in a furnace, a sound that slurs and slumps, breaks off and picks up again with wicked suddenness, and passes to the tricky clipping of the strings, rises to ferocity, then clouds and falls away into a blank carnal sadness. It is the music of the sexual act. Hungarians are more critical of the facility of the music than we are. I heard of one old man who refused to pay any orchestra unless they made him cry. He was experienced and resistant. He was angry if he beat them. But if they forced tears out of him, he paid them highly. They make a point of playing to lovers and, of course, come close enough to play pretty well under a girl's chin. The fiddler in one garden café set out to hypnotize a girl who was quarrelling with her young man. He put every trick he knew into his playing, and the orchestra played with its thunders and insinuations at the other end of the garden, backing him up but never looking at him. But, in the end, the girl and the young man simply ignored him, and without a sign on his face he went away. The performance had taken twenty minutes.

There was a tale going round Budapest when I was there that a Hungarian had volunteered to go by sputnik to the moon. When he was asked why he wanted to go to the moon, he said that he didn't want to, but that he had put in his application because he thought it might be a way of getting a sight of Vienna on the way. Hungarians crave to go to Vienna. It is very difficult to go. They would like to go to the Adriatic, but that is next to impossible: Yugoslavia is deviationist. Some do make the long journey across Romania and Bulgaria to the Black Sea. Hungary is lucky in Lake Balaton, and it shares the Neusiedler See with

79

Austria. Lake Balaton is one of the largest lakes in Europe; it reminds one of Lake Leman at Geneva, and tens of thousands go there for their holidays in the summer. The vines grow on the hills along the lakes; the villas, the hotels, the trades-union hostels, on the south side the pleasant, very southern-style towns—almost Provençal—make it a delightful little Riviera. Hundreds of white sails slope in the regattas, the white lake steamers ply up and down on the blue water and hoot to get the famous echo off the hills. When they hear the echo, all Hungarians are supposed to recite some lines of a famous patriotic poem which mean: "Don't leave your native land; it is a good place to live and die in."

I went out to Balaton by train, which takes about two hours. Like most train journeys in Hungary, this was a ride through flat, irrigated country, a graceful mixture of meadow, marsh, scrub, and cornland. The maize was ripening. Miles and miles of sunflowers were drooping, their seeds almost ready to be collected for the making of sunflower oil. (It is a cooking oil, and I think there is a lot to be said for the Hungarian belief that it is better than olive oil.) The heavy, narrow, horse-drawn carts were going down the dusty roads; now and then, one saw a man stripped to the waist and cutting corn with a scythe and women crossing the fields with mattocks on their shoulders. Tractors and combines are not very commonly seen except on the collective farms. Among the grassy banks the godetia was growing, larger and pinker than I have ever seen in northern Europe. The villages were scattered collections of red boxes, and occasionally, in a poor village, they were still thatching the roofs with rushes. There were long stretches where stooks of dark rushes were drying in the fields; for a moment, one mistakes them for stooks of very dark corn. Rushes are excellent insulators; in one of the Balaton villages, I saw a very large hut of rushes like a beehive; it was the communal refrigerator. Food can be kept cold or frozen in these simple mounds for months on end. The vines growing in the red soil by the lake looked in excellent order, and already, in some, the grapes were gathered and the rejoicings, the music, the dancing, had begun. The rocky peninsulas going out into the lake were almost Mediterranean; the poplar trees were grouped exactly to suggest the cypress of the south; the older houses in the towns were deep-walled.

I travelled with a cheerful, hustling collection of well-dressed men and women who were going to a weekend bridge tournament—bridge is still a strong Hungarian taste—but my own companion was an energetic and exalted young man whose interests were Gypsies and painting. He had worked for a dance band in the difficult times; he was interesting because he had been brought up as a Protestant. Nearly 30 per cent of Hungarians belong to the Lutheran Church, and they have been noted, as a sect, for producing outstanding figures. There is an interesting colony of painters at Balaton. I did not see any examples of Socialist Realism in their work. They are a hospitable lot, and one or two have lovely old houses in which one finds the high green or brown or white and gold tiled stoves, as monumental as shrines, in the corner of the room. Out come the little cups of coffee the moment the visitor arrives. Later, the white wine and delicious little things to eat. I always find painters better company than writers; they have more curiosity and observe more things. These painters did not complain of anything much except that they were starved for Paris. The real difficulty for the State is that it accumulates large quantities of paintings which it does not know what to do with. Like the Poles, the Hungarian painters are being tactfully diverted towards handicrafts, folk arts, and decorative work, and with some deplorable success.

I stayed in a hillside village on Balaton. It was a hot little place of rocky paths and lanes ankle-deep in dust and loose stone, with pigs, and pullets scampering about, and geese on the march. The gardens were full of showy dahlias. There were strong girls at the washtubs and at the wells. I stayed in a little bungalow owned by a kindly widow, and slept in a bedroom that contained the usual wedding photographs and religious lithograph over the bedhead. Someone in the house was a great reader of paperbacks. My friend and I ate our dinner of roast pork and sauerkraut very late that night at a labourer's tavern which had its own Gypsy in attendance. He played on the rough terrace where we were eating, and the labourers shouted compliments and insults to him as he played. He had a cigarette in his stained fingers all the time as he played, and he took no notice of what was said. Someone brought him a drink afterwards. He merely nodded. He was a thin, poor, nervous Gypsy with bloodshot eyes who lived in the village and was pitied because he had been the victim of a loose-living wife who had caused him trouble. That night when I groped my way over the stones and boulders in the dark to the bungalow, I was alarmed to be barked at and followed around by twenty or thirty excited dogs who rushed out of the shadows. They had been on the chain all day: the villagers turn them out at night to fight and work off their energy. All night long they squabbled and barked at the moon.

Back in Budapest, I found I had to fly south again to Pécs. I wanted to see an industrial town and Pécs has coal mines, and not far off are the uranium mines. The uranium —to the annoyance of Hungarians—goes to Russia. A wild Hungarian horse fair takes place every year near Pécs, but I missed it. The little Malev planes—Malev is the State Airline—can take about ten passengers, but there were only an engineer and a couple of peasants on the flight with me. We fluttered along until we got to the densely wooded hills and saw the sad, wide Danube sketching its way up to the hazy skyline in long bends towards Belgrade. The Turks got to Pécs, and there is a mosque—now an ornate Catholic church—in the main square. There is also a pretty little minaret standing in the backyard of a brewery. The town is old, very busy, very noisy, and pretty. It has a university and it is famous for its ceramics. An automatic harmonium playing "Come Back to Sorrento" and "O Sole Mio" with the pedal down spread its treacly sounds from an empty café under the trees in the main square. For the rest, Pécs is an old steep place of little shops and little one-storey houses, like a town in the South of Spain. There are old ladies and girls at the windows, the sewing machines are going (these sewing rooms are unsocialized); the tailors sit on their tables, the little cafés fill up when the workers swarm in by bus in the evenings, and the hairdressers work late. There were stacks of black watermelons like cannon balls in the streets. An opera company had lately done *Otello* in the town. During the rush hour I watched the newspaper seller standing in the main square, with stacks of the evening paper, but I saw no one buy one from him. The Hungarians are avid and instructed readers and are terribly bored by their official press. The only papers they like are the picture papers and the literary weeklies. The industrial part of Pécs is a couple of miles away. The workers are very well housed. The lack of coal in Hungary has been a national problem for generations, and there is no doubt about it that the State looks after the miners, who may not be highly paid, but do better than other workers. The failure in housing elsewhere was a good deal responsible for the anger of the masses in 1956.

I stayed in an old-fashioned hotel in Pécs, a place where everything was outsize, from the quantities of indoor plants in the old glass-enclosed corridors to the immense beds, quilts, sofas, and wardrobes in the bedroom. I fancy I got the bridal suite, which outdid in Germanic carving anything I have ever seen. The State unloads its oil paintings on the hotels; my room had four or five very large, violently coloured original paintings: reaping scenes, vineyards, and portraits of powerful peasants. The scene in the dining room in the evening was a replica of what one sees in all the solid provincial hotels in the world. Somebody's small jazz orchestra played to the melancholy middle-aged men—businessmen, officials, each sitting alone at his table before a carnation in a silver-plated vase. One or two couples danced. Except for the nightly dancing, one might have been sitting in Troyes in France or Andover in England. I was with a middle-aged man who had something to do with libraries and who was still sentimental about his days in London before the war. We played the game of spotting the Party members and working out their life stories. In these places, he said, it was easy to spot them.

"That young couple over there, dancing very stiffly," he said. "The young man with the earnest look of a deputy assistant manager in an electrical-supply company—his wife with glasses, the scrubbed look, and her hair as tight as her lips, and the air of an English Sunday-school teacher —that is the type. Let us see if they ever smile."

They did not.

The general tone of the Party is puritan, priggish, earnest, and sentimental. It is always lecturing and rebuking. It sees itself as a genteel and dedicated minority, and there is no doubt that in education, for example, they have raised the general standard dramatically as far as the three *R*'s and simple technical education are concerned. In other departments education is in a state of political crisis. Children are very well cared for and look healthy. On the whole, Europe has always preferred the disciplined child to the child that "expresses" itself. But the Party sees the whole of life as a school, and the mass of people hate that. I was amused by the crowd at the railway station at Pécs. The country people piled into the waiting hall and camped there with their basketloads of yellow peppers, their bursting bunches of dahlias, their bundles of salami sandwiches, their cakes and their beer, enjoying the heat, the uproar, the mess, and the reek of poor humanity. Next door, in what is called the Culture Waiting Room, which has a few sad pieces of framed and educative peasant embroidery on the wall, were sitting three middle-aged ladies, spotless, prim, silent—Party members of Victorian respectability, holier than the crowds next door.

Drastic societies like the Communist produce their special kind of corruption. With his carelessness and intelligence, the Hungarian is quick to find ways of getting around the regulations. The traveller's voucher system in the hotels is easily manipulated. Then it is a country where "influence" and personal arrangements are indispensable. before 1956, the Government went much too far in forcible collectivization; they have had to retreat—for the moment. You can own a house or a flat of not more than six rooms now, and people with large houses can now let them. This is in fact a scandal, for the State took over these large houses and has now been driven to reselling them—but not to the original owners! People who are called "class enemies" and their children have a bad time. This leads to strong feelings. Miss X, daughter of a class enemy, wishes to follow evening class at the University; the way is barred. She asks Mr. Y, who has the ear of the authority, to wangle permission. In exchange, she uses her influence with the engineers to see that Mr. Y gets that almost impossible thing, a telephone. This particular intrigue took a new turn when I was in Budapest. The postman had intervened and offered to get the telephone order fixed up, for a *douceur* of 1,000 fiorints! I do not say that Hungarians are more corrupt than other people; they are just easygoing, especially about money. I do say that Communist states are as corrupt as others, and that there is more confusion in them, and that the corruption exists in the Party. Where did that car come from? How did you get that flat? One of the cleverest and most gossipy populations in the world knows very well.

Many people, indeed most people, deny that Communism has raised the standard of life among the masses, but I do not see how this can be judged. There is a general rise in the standard of living, health, and education throughout Europe; a new class has emerged and dominates: the lower middle class. If they had nationalized the largest industrial concerns, let the farmers and peasants alone, after breaking up the large estates, and kept their hands off the shops, the Communist governments would not have a sullen, grudging people on their hands. But Communism has done away with dire poverty. The scandals of Sicily and Calabria have no parallel in the satellite countries. Remove Russian troops and pressure, and the natural liberality of a deeply Western people would once more assert itself; there seems little hope of that happening.

I left these gay, intelligent, and hospitable people with regret. Their gaiety concealed the apprehension in their lives; their cynicism was the mask of courage. Though many of them are pestered and working themselves to death under bad conditions, they brighten at the growing signs of a better life, and they know how to live. I promised to return, and it is one of the countries I would like very much to go back to. But it is always with a feeling of relief that the traveller leaves these places, picks up his first Western paper on the international plane, and knows he does not have to worry about what he says and about getting people into trouble with the police. One is excited once more to see the brilliant lights of Austria, Germany, Belgium, and Holland come up under the wings of the plane. The trim red roofs of the Austrian cities, the green Danube coiling, look reassuring when one has left the land of anxiety.

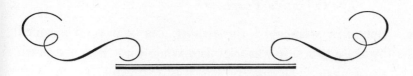

BULGARIA

In the last afternoon hours of the flight from Vienna eastward over the rusting Austrian forests, Europe looked emptier. Even a large town—was it Niš?—seemed tiny. High mountain ranges rose about us, and this gave the illusion that the plane was trudging a lonely course over them and was going slower. We passed into darkness. Then the moon rose, and when the lights of Sofia appeared after a couple of hours, they suggested a scattered city of deserted countrified streets. Again illusion: Sofia is small, modern, and compact.

We were on the last flight of the day, and when we arrived we sat freezing in the airport bus for an hour while they closed the airport and the staff got aboard. Some flighty Arab traveller tried a few jokes with the stout

Bulgarian women of the airport, but was soon silenced by these ladies. It was very late when I got into my hotel, the Balkan. The autumn air was hard and frosty. This hotel was vast and sumptuous and almost empty. There was nothing to read but official booklets. No one came into the bar except an occasional pair of Lufthansa pilots who played the jukebox and drank caraway-flavoured gin. It took me some time to understand that when a Bulgarian shakes his head in a negative movement he means "Yes" and the up-and-down nod means "No."

Another oddity of life in Bulgaria is linguistic. A large number of people have a smattering of German, a hangover from the war and from pre-war contacts with Germany; a few speak French; very young employees sometimes speak excellent English. The oddity is that quite a few of them speak Spanish. I am not sure why. In the dining room at the Balkan, two men at the next table, a Bulgarian and a very polished Spaniard, were discussing in Castilian how thoroughly the Communists were now organized in the Spanish vineyards.

These dining-room scenes in the satellite countries are always interesting. At the Balkan there was an English engineer who was putting in the equipment for the new television station and who complained that he was always followed by spies and had angrily made a fuss with the authorities. They denied that he was followed. There was a Fernandel-like Bulgarian who gave lavish dinner parties. His gaiety vanished when he saw the bill and his face went through every expression of anxiety, impatience, disclaimer, self-satisfaction, until, with inexpressible relief, he got the receipt he could show to the accounts department at his office. Many people ordered tea, which came in pretty little pots. I ordered a glass of wine and was asked if I wanted 200 grammes. There was a pestiferous Romanian who worked the hotels, drawing portraits. "They are great art," he said. Two terrible pictures of moonlight over the Black Sea saddened the dining room. In a cafeteria nearby, people wrapped up in jerseys or leather jackets listened to old-fashioned French tunes on the wireless. Haunting the hotel for several days was an elegant American woman who was collecting folk music: she was excited by the fine choral singing in the country.

In the autumn mornings there is a freezing white fog which creeps over Sofia until eleven o'clock. I used to watch the scene from the hotel. On one side of the square was the Greek Orthodox church, its bells very noisy at sundown; on the other a Turkish mosque and the baths; near them the big new store called Zoum, a crowded low-class emporium of shoddy goods. I had to join a queue to buy a notebook. The shirts and socks were poor; all textiles were scarce; shoes for children had not existed for a fortnight. The press was very angry about this. Outside was a model of a new "People's Car," not for sale, which was admired by groups of men all day. By now perhaps the motor age has arrived, but when I was there Sofia was almost without cars and but for the crowded old-fashioned trams which start running at about five in the morning, the city was beautifully quiet. Ponies and mules trotted by, drawing rubber-tyred carts with loads of bricks and timber. Outside the block of flats, wood was being sawn up against the winter. Men were hammering away in the coopers' yards; peppers were hanging to dry on the walls. One often sees the sheepskin jacket and the thonged leather slippers with pointed toes worn, I believe, in Macedonia. But modern life intervenes in the peasant mixture: pedestrian crossings had been marked out and the police were in force obliging the people to use them —an abstract exercise. Old peasant women were experts at feigning deafness at the sound of the police whistles. Communist countries are like schools: the population is trained and, like school children, have their own ways of getting around authority. There was a meat shortage in Sofia when I was there, due (it was said) to the export of meat to Turkey, but the better-off Bulgarians got their meat by tipping the butcher—in short, the British rationing system. Some of the windows of Zoum were painted over in white: this indicated a storeroom for cloth, and the gossip was that cloth costing 200 leva in the shops could be had at 60 by members of the Party. Life for the mass of people, in short, was an ingenious battle for things, and some private trade is still permitted in the country markets. A quick-thinking professor I was with one day, bought lemons off a private dealer in the market at Plovdiv to resell at a very high price in Sofia! At the Palace of Justice there is always a crowd of people, many of them peasants, who have gone there to settle the disputes that arise from the bonus system on which wages are paid on the collective farms. A large amount of time is spent by the population in finding their way, legally, illegally, or semi-legally, in a system which is difficult enough for the planners, but often mysterious for the planned. A British Communist who had settled in Bulgaria said that 60 per cent or even more of the population were opposed to the system, but they were learning to live with it. Why not? Human beings are ingenious and the conditions of life were improving. In Western Europe there is general ignorance of Bulgaria. The only knowledgeable people I found in London before I went were a few British Communists who had discovered the attractions of the country, its wild landscape, its charming towns, and its good red wine.

There is an underlying elation in Bulgarian life even though the mass of the people may be merely acquiescent in Communism. The elation goes back to the nineteenth century. Bulgaria is only eighty-eight years old—all the Balkan states are "young." The regard for Russia is rooted in history, for the Russians liberated Bulgaria from the Turks in the 1870's, though complete legal freedom dates only from 1908. So the break with the past which Communist countries insist on really occurred long before the last war, indeed in the nineteenth century and, since the Turkish hegemony was long, the Bulgarians still feel the exhilaration of national freedom. As in Poland and Hungary, the strongest feeling is national, and to the Bulgarians there is the additional stimulus of having obtained religious freedom—though oddly they are not a religious people. The general temperament has been sceptical for centuries. The Moslems oppressed and the Greek Orthodox Church, which was and has been the custodian of national culture in Greece, was hostile to the cultural revival of Bulgaria, which indeed prospered because it was anti-Greek. There were never any great feudal estates outside of a few owned by the monasteries; the peasants have lived for generations on eighteen-acre holdings. It was common in some parts of the country to find the *zadruga*, or house community, in which several dozen people lived in family groups and worked together on one farm.

When the white fog lifts and the morning sparkles, one realizes that Sofia is a mountain city. It is 1,700 feet above sea level. Thickly wooded mountains and flashing snow peaks look down on it. The heat is violent in the summer; there is a long, very vivid, warm autumn, and the winter is severe. Sofia is an exhilarating and pretty place of dozens of parks and gardens. There are fine avenues of poplars, the tallest I have seen in Europe. At the beginning of the century it was a very provincial place of 80,000 inhabitants; now it has 600,000. One comes across many middle-aged people who can remember when the centre of the city was a warren of unpaved lanes with horses neighing and cattle lowing in them. The war caused great damage, but that has been repaired. One has the impression of a place built of stone. Some of the main streets are paved with a pleasant yellowish glazed cobblestone that seems to bring the sunlight to one's feet. The main roads that run out of the city are planted with mile after mile of roses —for this is the country of the attar. They grow in beds under the acacias in the towns.

The pace of life is slow. The crowds in the street were solemn and well wrapped up against the cold; it was a homely peasant crowd. But I soon found myself among more interesting company. The country is not rich, and the office worker often works in modest premises, and

94

the officials were, on the whole, shabby. They reminded me of the Portuguese—hairy people with heavy eyebrows and strong proud faces, obliging, lively, candid, sceptical men of considerable lazy dignity; the women plain, inelegant, but spontaneous, good-natured, and affectionate. The city dwellers are not highly paid and they have to work hard. On my first Sunday I was alone. There was a tram station near the hotel where hundreds of people were queuing for the trams, fighting their way to the ticket window. I joined the fight. There we all were, soldiers, peasants, hikers, the Bulgarian crowd. I had been told to get the tram up to the pretty village of Boyana in the mountains and to visit a little church which had fine thirteenth-century murals. The Bulgarians love walking, camping, going to the mountains; they love country life. They put on their rucksacks, pick up their sticks, and start off. I got onto the tram. Later I had to change to one of those old mountain trams where you hang on to the step as best you can.

"Boyana? Boyana?" I shouted.

Immediately a strong arm pulled me and a heavy shoulder butted me aboard. We were all jammed chest to chest. The puller spoke a little German. When I said I came from London, several voices exclaimed with delight: "B.B.C." The friendly memory of the wartime broadcasts of the B.B.C. is strong all over Europe. Another man struggled through the squash towards me and started kissing me and—when we had more room—hugging me too. In between kisses, he shouted in German to the whole tramload of us: "All men are brothers, all over the world." It was his only German sentence. In ten minutes, the two of them forced me off the tram, kissed and hugged me now freely in the street, and took me to their house. For the rest of the afternoon I was their miracle and showpiece, gazed at, even stroked. At one moment they danced round me. I am sixty years old, grey, and very bald. I mention my age because I found myself venerated because of it.

Our talk was hardly conversation, but like a game of cards with nouns for trumps in French, German, and English. One of the men was a printer, sharp and intense; the other a very thin emotional innocent, a lithographer, he said, "in six colours." They lived in part of a patched-up villa with broken railings. The poorly furnished sitting room had two iron beds in it, also a stove and a sink. A very sick young man, a relation, was there eating a sad little mess of food in tomato sauce. In the entrance porch was another bed. The pretty wife of one of them stood stiff with astonishment, gazing, with her little girl hiding her head in her mother's skirt. Presently the woman brought glasses of water for us on a tin tray and a little bowl of cherry preserve.

"Taste it. Drink it," they both shouted. "The water of the Balkan! It is the best water in the world."

For "Balkan" is the general name for mountain, as well as being the name of one of the great mountain ranges of this country. It was beautiful water. Afterwards, people in Sofia were always saying: "Have you drunk our water? What do you think of it?" I became an addict. I have never tasted water like it, except in Spain. Our palates have been corrupted by the chemically treated and so-called "pure" water of our cities.

We sat stammering, knee to knee.

"How much does a printer earn in London?"

"Here," they said, "800 leva a month." (Say, £30 at the tourist rate of exchange, but that has no real meaning.)

"It is very little," the sharper one said. "But here we have a special system," he said with a mixture of wonder and enthusiasm. "It is called the Communist system? Are you a capitalist?"

"Yes," I said.

The simpler of the two listened painfully. He had a set of steel teeth which gave him an official and ferocious look. He had the flat face of a Byzantine saint. He didn't understand a word we were saying: he uttered his chorus: "All men are brothers. All over the world." Every time our nouns and infinitives failed and we were reduced to the pathos of dumb animals, he started up ecstatically: "All men are brothers." It was rather fine. Then he would give me another kiss, and we were all laughing. We left the house and went, climbing and climbing, with the crowds of Sunday hikers into the golden trees. The printers shouted to passers-by about their capture. People stopped to talk to us. The Bulgarians are very gregarious.

"Walk between us," they said. "You are older than we are and we wish to show you respect. How old are you?"

I told them.

"Do you know how old he is?" they shouted to passers-by. "He is an Englishman. He is sixty."

"If you are as old as that," the sharp one said, "do not walk so fast."

"So you are really a capitalist!" the sharper one repeated.

97

"Yes," I said. "I must be. I own a one-pound share in a company."

He explained again to his friend with the steel teeth, who hugged my shoulders and laughed into my eyes.

"All men are brothers!" he shouted. "All over the world."

Travel soon turns one into a figure of ridicule.

From Boyana there is a fine view of the immense valley that opens in the clear air below the mountains of Vitosha. The distant city stands out hard pink and white, rather like Madrid, and at this time of the year the turning leaves of the trees were fiery. The little church at Boyana is hidden under trees. It is a tiny place of three chapels, the oldest part built in the eleventh century with a nave six yards long and a central cupola. Another chapel was added in the thirteenth century and yet another in the nineteenth. But the frescoes are the thing. They date from the thirteenth century. They anticipate the beginning of the Italian Renaissance by several decades. The chief portraits are of Kaloyan, the feudal lord who built the middle chapel, and his bride, and the artist has broken away from the austere canons of Byzantine art. Bulgaria is rich in religious painting.

The printers had often seen the frescoes, and they pointed out their beauties again and again. Presently an English-speaking couple joined us—and explained in detail to the printers who I was and what I did. It was a little sad to see they felt they had lost something of their miracle now that it could be explained to them. We all walked back down the rough mountain road together. The last

98

sunflowers were seeding, the maize stalks stood in the gardens, and, lower down, the fields of strawberries began.

That night I went to the opera. There are four opera companies in Bulgaria, and in this genre the Bulgarians excel, for they are fine singers. The best are trained in Italy and are known all over Europe. Unluckily the best singers were in Vienna at this time, but it was not the fault of the performers that I found *War and Peace* rather dull. It is a patriotic work, and it ends with tremendous mass singing by the Partisans of the Napoleonic campaign, for the theme of the Partisan—though wearing thin in the eyes of the younger generation in Bulgaria—was still popular. This opera is good picture-book stuff and rather more like a Spanish *zarzuela* than grand opera. I had fallen into intellectual company by now. I had made friends with a personable and cheerful young man who enjoyed life. He spoke excellent English and had just finished translating the whole of Shelley into Bulgarian—one line of Shelley, he said, took two lines of Bulgarian. I have often seen him in London since: he was considering translating *Paradise Lost*! He was not a Party member but he was a strong Marxist. He reminded me of the English Marxists of the thirties. He was very emphatic about the Oriental character of Bulgarian life: Asia and Turkey cast their light on it. If he had been less loyal in his politics he would have had to admit that Greek influence had been strong.

"It is no joke being a writer under Communism," he said when we first met. "One is always being ordered to entertain and educate some foreign visitor. You never get any time to yourself." At the Writers' or Journalists'

Union, one talks over a glass or two of raspberry brandy. One talks, but feels embarrassed by meetings which can have no intimacy. One eminent historical novelist in an official position made a vehement propaganda speech reciting the increases in production in everything from fertilizers upwards and announced that, whereas Calabrian recruits for the Italian army were all illiterate, in Bulgaria 60 per cent of the recruits had received secondary education. The sales of serious Bulgarian and foreign literature are, of course, very large indeed. He was a bulky man with a fine rugged head, bold nose, bushy eyebrows, and sly humorous eyes, very much the old novelist with a trilogy behind him and admired (I found) because he was "a true Bulgarian type," very sceptical under his domineering assurance. He complained that some of the younger generation were still "looking for a style and getting lost." He was predictably anti-American—"American literature has so little"—and said American writers had no influence; his view was due to ignorance; he was voicing official policy. The fact is that Hemingway, Faulkner, and Steinbeck are translated and their influence has been as powerful in Bulgaria as it has been in its time in the rest of Europe, East and West. Only out-of-date old Stalinists embarrass the young by going on and on about *Hamlet*, Shaw, and Galsworthy. The splendid old man had just not kept up. He belonged to the generation which turned to the writing of historical novels—it was safer—and to the stories of the Partisans.

Some of the young were indignant about the criticism that they were "looking for a style" and were "lost." The thaw had not gone far in Bulgaria; Socialist Realism was still the thing. But a real conflict between the generations had begun. This does not mean that they are anti-Communist. Indeed, they regard Communism as an elastic, organic changing way of life rather than a rigid doctrine. Of course they have "troubles" and "difficulties" and "delays." The most interesting Bulgarian painter—I did not catch his name—has not been allowed to exhibit since 1940. The theatre, I was told apologetically, is very poor. On the other hand, the poets are said to do better. This was our chatter on one or two evenings when we sat having dinner at the old Russian Officers' Club, drinking the powerful *slivovitz*—the plum- or pine-tinctured spirit—and the red wine, smoking the excellent cigarettes from the Rhodope tobacco fields. Our food had a strong Turkish bias, but we ate superb smoked salmon, thick and dark in colour and kept in sunflower oil; good pork, lamb, and herb sausages. The Club dates from the liberation of the 1870's, and with its red curtains, its lace, its glass screens, and its old attentive waiters—about the best in my Eastern European journeys—it suggested an old-fashioned set for a play by Chekhov. It is about the only restaurant that escapes from the awful grandiose negligence of the hotels where one waits and waits in vain for food to come, and that has not, like others, gone downhill to the level of the popular cafeteria.

There was one tough-looking, gay young novelist who talked Spanish. "We are exactly like the Spaniards," he said. "They had the Moors. We had the Turks. And we have the same feeling for personal dignity and masculinity."

"And puritanism too?" I asked.

"Oh God," he exclaimed. "We are the most puritan

race in Europe. It isn't Stalinist puritanism. It has nothing
to do with the Party. It is in the bones. People here speak
of Romania as if they were going to hell. For us Romania
is the red-light district of Eastern Europe. We are very
severe. In the villages a woman could be imprisoned for
adultery. If you go to a hotel with your wife, you are quite
likely to be to asked to show your marriage license. A
few months ago I was walking down the street outside this
restaurant with my arm round my wife's waist. We were
laughing loudly. A policeman came up and told me to remove my arm from her waist. Then he told her to take
my arm and walk decorously. This puritanism has nothing
to do with religion, because the Greek Church has little
influence, and never has had. We have never had a strong
religious sense, and the despots we have lived under have
turned us into sceptics. But these puritan waves sweep
over us from time to time. One year they sweep all the
lovers out of the parks in the summer; next year it dies
down and the lovers go back again."

My friends were sorry about this and, as far as I could
tell, had no serious political troubles in their lives. But
one does hear, of course, of political miseries. There was
young and clever Mrs. X, who was just divorced. During
the legal examination, her maiden name came to light.
It revealed that she was related to one of the condemned
men in a notorious political trial a great many years back.
She had become suspect at once and was certain that she
would lose her job and find the greatest difficulty in getting
another.

"I just live from day to day," she said. Especially among

the spirited and gifted, there are people in all these countries who are in the sort of jam so many Americans got into during the McCarthy period.

She was a thin, shabby woman with dyed red hair, hard and plain as a good many Bulgarian women are, but she was attractive when she laughed. She was an amusing talker and worked hard, as they all do.

The mountain scenery of Bulgaria is spectacular. The northern frontier is the Danube and its plain; south of this is the Balkan range, then a valley, warm and subtropical, opens out, getting wider and wider until it reaches the Black Sea: south of the plain rise the superb Rhodope Mountains, and along their crest lies the frontier with Greece. I drove out to the mountain resort outside Sofia among the fiery autumn trees and watched the school children dancing and singing in their open-air classes and sat out in the sun with the cheerful family parties. We drank a glass of *pastis*—the Greek *ouzo*—ate cucumbers and tomatoes—for this, as they say, is the season of the pickle jars—and ate veal soup, pork kebab in paprika sauce, and quantities of grapes. The wasps buzzed around. The modern hotels and resort restaurants are very good. One might have been in the Guadarrama in Spain. Later on I drove to Plovdiv, the second-largest town in the country, lying in the hot, dusty plain, and went to a couple of collective farms. Plovdiv is some eighty or ninety miles southeast of Sofia on the excellent international road to Istanbul. There is little traffic on it.

We got down from the frosty cold of Sofia into the hot and lazy airs of the plain, and we drove down the long straight avenues of yellow poplars, beeches, and oaks blazing in wild madders, ochres, scarlets, and gold. It was like driving tens of miles through fire. In the sunny haze, the tall yellow trees seem to be floating or dancing on the blue mountains, and the light is strong. And, mile after mile under the trees, the roses were in flower. It was a landscape of black soil where the maize had been cut. The streets of the little towns on the way were packed with country people wandering about under the acacias in the streets; and under the acacias, once more, the roses.

One of the collective farms occupied the land of four villages with a population of 10,000 people. The villages themselves are scattered collections of two-storey red-brick houses with long deep porches. The older houses are covered with vines. The headquarters of the collective was in one of these houses at a crossroads. Motor bicycles and bikes were propped against the wall in a strong smell of silage. (They chop up maize stalks for this, pasturage being poor on the plains.) The head of the collective was an official, I suppose a Party member, not from this neighborhood; but he had local assistants: warm, huge-fisted farmers who gave one a crushing hand grip and looked one fearlessly in the eye in a manly fashion. The offices of the collectives are always the same. There is a simple desk where the chief sits, with a row of agricultural books on it. There is a table covered with red baize and with a jug of water and a fly whisk. On the wall there is a picture of Lenin—busts of Lenin and Stalin are in a large number of Bulgarian offices and shops; Khrushchev is less often seen. The chief did not lecture me, but in practical fashion got out his papers with all the figures written in longhand on them and answered questions. The labour force, he said, was 3,500 men and women. The farm grew grain, a variety of flax, wheat, tomatoes, and apples. It had 5,000 sheep—the British have been sending breeding stock—350 cows, 30,000 hens, and 1,500 pigs. The farm hired its machinery from a State pool. (They were delighted by the machine milker.) This farm was proud of having fulfilled its grain quota—half of the unrest among satellite peasants is caused by putting delivery quotas too high, especially to discourage the uncollectivized —and also of having beaten the Italians that season in the rush for the tomato market in Vienna. Another farm I visited had done the same, but confessed that they had not, in their enthusiasm, learned to make sound tomato boxes as the Italians do. The Turks buy their meat. It is impossible to say what real wages are, but the average annual earning of a worker, I was told, is 14,000 leva (the tourist rate is 27 to the pound, certainly an over-valuation), and the worker is paid in a series of advances of 500 leva through part of the year and collects the balance at the end. His normal rate is on the basis of a low norm called a working day, but in fact any day he is likely to work more than his norm, and is paid accordingly. Later on in Sofia, when I was asking what kind of lawsuits came on at the court, I was told that the favourite court case is a dispute of a worker or peasant with the State organization about the calculations of hours and pay. This kind of dispute is always protracted.

There was a fine, rugged, shaggy-haired farmer of about fifty sitting with us in the office of the collective. He sat swatting flies which swarmed in the sticky air, and he had sly, shrewd, laughing peasant eyes. I asked him what difference he had found between this system of farming here and the one he had grown up in. He said: "We never had big estates in Bulgaria—well, except for one or two large demesnes belonging to the monasteries of the Orthodox Church. There were one or two big farmers, a lot of medium farmers, and then the rest—poor fellows living on eighteen acres, some of it rich in the market-garden areas, some poor. Although they were poor, they could live. On the whole, life has always been good in this country."

"You say you prefer the collective farm to the private system?" I said. "Why?"

His answer was shrewd.

"Under the private system," he said, "if a farmer has a good year and has money in his pocket, he has only one idea—to buy more land. Land has always been the peasant's passion. He buys land at the expense of his house, his family, and the pleasures of life. In the collectives you can't buy land, so you spend money on your home and family, furnish it better. You take seaside holidays."

This collective made its own wine, enough to supply a litre a day free to everyone. The juice was bubbling away in huge vats in an open barn. There was a pretty country house nearby, and obviously the vineyard and presses had belonged once to a comfortable private family who had laid out pretty gardens under the trees—what had become of them? The man in charge was middle-aged and had the high seriousness the art always brings out, and when we sat at a stone table under the trees drinking a glass or two, he said, in the tone of a true connoisseur, that his

wine had something of Moulin-à-Vent in it. He was not far
wrong. It turned out that he had been sent to Dijon to learn
the trade when he was a young man and, until then, like
all good Bulgarians, thought that the water of the Balkans
was superior to any liqueur. He had been horribly shocked
when his French landlady had brought him a bowl of
water to wash in: he thought it sacrilege to *wash* in water!
This raised a question I did not care to ask. The vintner was
a travelled worker of the old school. Afterwards the friend
who had come with me said: "Did you notice he described
himself as a technician? It's the new vanity here. Everyone
likes to be called a technician now. Even Silenus would call
himself a technician if he were reborn in Bulgaria."

We drove round over fields and rough roads. We visited
several houses occupied by farm workers. Perhaps they
were showplaces. Except for the absence of things like
refrigerators and washing machines, they were modest new
villas or bungalows such as one sees in suburban Britain or
America, well furnished, with a standard contemporary
wallpaper on the wall, good beds, cots for the children,
spotlessly clean. One I especially liked. The basement was
used for storage and down some steps we saw a huge tub
filled with fermenting wine. Tending it stood the delinquent
old uncle of the family, bottle-nosed, limping "because he
didn't feel so well today." It was his second barrel this year,
he said; he had already drunk most of the first. He obviously
did not restrict himself to the farm's free litre. He told me
this furtively, under the vines that were trellised over the
little yard, and with a sly glance at his disapproving relations. He took us on a poetic visit to each branch of the

vines, telling us which grapes were the best. Grandfather was there, a blue-eyed and soldierly old man with white moustaches fit for an Emperor of the old regime, who said he hoped I had not come with a bomb in my pocket and was a man of peace. At this his grandchild, a baby in arms, threw its china doll at me and smashed it.

"It's all right for us. We don't want war. We've had enough. But you'll have to keep an eye on the younger generation," he said to his daughter-in-law.

On another farm the girls were packing the apples and tomatoes in the sheds, and one stout old lady marched up and asked did I want world peace—it is the stock political question put to all foreigners, indicating how they have been taught to believe they live in a hostile world. The very words they used in their work show it: they speak of tomato-packing brigades, sabotage—if something goes wrong—shock workers, etc., etc., and there are always posters showing capitalist soldiers, usually American, in tanks shooting down Chinese, Vietnamese, and Korean peasants. The Partisans are glorified, and indeed the general atmosphere of siege reminded me of Britain during the Second World War. A war atmosphere is maintained to make them feel that their system is engaged in a daily battle. But in the packing sheds there was laughing good nature. They like a joke, and at the end of the day I found myself in a broken-down shed drinking with three sinful old men who were distilling a ferocious raw apple spirit like Calvados.

We drove off in the dust as the women were coming in from the fields with mattocks on their shoulders, fine creatures in bunched-out skirts and with white scarves on their heads; some young men were just finishing off a new football stadium and cinder track which had the usual large portrait of Lenin and another of a hero of the Resistance on the gate. There was a House of Culture where they held socials and saw films. Our guide was a huge peasant, and very proud. We overtook his own sheep being driven home in the evening, for each man is allowed a bit of land for himself, five sheep, a cow, and a few hens, which he can sell. There are always private traders in the street markets—my host was extravagant enough to pay 25 leva for five lemons in the market at Plovdiv. The only blot on this collective—in the farmer's opinion but not in mine—was the tumbledown colony of the Gypsy camp. The long red sunset was colouring the fields of maize, and the Rhodope Mountains had turned hard and purple; along a track came one of these Gypsy youths singing, with his scythe on his shoulder.

"I don't understand these people," the farmer said angrily. "Once they've got a bit of a money they stop work and sing and dance and drink and fight and gamble and won't work until it's gone. They won't move into the new houses. We must move them out." Occasionally Gypsies produce a first-class doctor or lawyer.

"Or, in Spain, a bullfighter or a dancer," I said. He was very shocked, as any successful farmer is if you praise a Gypsy.

The city of Plovdiv is large and pretty, a place of acacias and flowers, lying on the steep bumpy hills of the Maritsa River land—the river that flows down to Greece.

Plovdiv has its modern side and is known for its international exhibitions. It has several mosques and some Turkish population. One of the hills is dominated by the enormous statue of a Russian soldier affectionately called Alyosha—the generic name for Russian soldiers. Plovdiv was a lazy, dusty, pleasant place. A troupe of Vietnam dancers came into the hotel carrying bunches of chrysanthemums—tiny people, delicate, thin, ill dressed, and pathetic beside the solid Bulgarians. Some twenty Party notabilities, looking like businessmen at a convention, were having a silent lunch together; one wondered who mistrusted whom. There are some fine examples of old boyar houses in the town—the boyars were the small gentry or nobles who were suborned or destroyed by the Turks. Many turned to the Moslem faith to escape the massacres and savageries of the time. The Bulgarians are proud that, in this century, they stopped the Nazis from sending the Bulgarian Jews to the gas chambers. The liberal spirit is fundamentally strong, but the Party officials go through contortions of silence or polite evasion if one praises Israel. There was a busy market in Plovdiv, under the trees, selling maize, flour, and such foods in sacks, saffron, herbs. Some were selling old oil lamps and loofahs. The fleece hat and the jodphur-like black or brown trousers with deep waist bands were common.

Now that the Mediterranean and the Adriatic are virtually closed to them, half the holiday makers of the Eastern European states make for the Black Sea, and especially for the Bulgarian resorts near Varna and the newer one south of it at Burgas. They have become a workers'

Riviera with the wealth and folly removed, bronzing and healthy and youthful, the reward of the sound citizen. Architecturally they are modern in the best sense. The sands are golden, and although connoisseurs find the water of the Black Sea sluggish and not buoyant enough, the wind hard, and the landscape of the coastal plain dull, there is no doubt about the placid enjoyment of the holiday life there. Travellers report that the Bulgarian quarter is far superior to the Crimea, which is all mass hostels and sanatoria. The Bulgarians have preserved a carousing spirit; the wine-drinking, sun-soaking nations always do. For myself the Bulgaria of the mountain towns and superb landscapes is more dramatic. Trnovo toppling down the sides of its gorges, with its strange murals of the fifteenth century, and the famous tenth-century monastery at Rila, which is a strange mixture of caravanserai and the religious life. I have met young women students from the West who have taken their motor bicycles to Bulgaria and have enjoyed every moment of their life with a hospitable people.

We drove back to Sofia in a comfortable Russian car. The cafés in the country towns were packed and roaring. Life there must have been what it always had been. If the main streets of Sofia were empty at night, the back streets were thronged. The crowd were strolling up and down in a *paseo* which recalled the habits, though not the electric animation, of the Spanish evenings. It was a family crowd. The streets were darkish, for neon lighting and lamps were few. There were dozens of tailors working late, the sewing machines humming away, the flatirons and presses thumping while the radio played music that had an Oriental note.

Many of the tailors squatted cross-legged on the tables. There were queues for fish. The hairdressers were crowded with women.

There was not much to do except to wander about staring at things. On Sunday there was a band and a procession marching to the tomb where Dimitrov is embalmed, guarded by smart goose-stepping soldiers. I wandered into the old and beautiful Nevsky Church and found what, in my ignorance, I can only call a cocktail party, going on before the choir, for there was a buffet there and the people were standing about eating cakes, sausages, and meat rolls. Since this is the most revered church in Sofia, I feel certain the occasion was religious. The modern cathedral, to which the Russians presented a golden dome, is a garish place, plastered with gaudy mosaics, eloquent of the decline of Christian art into poster-like and sentimental vulgarity.

I shall always remember the clean, leafy, mountainy smell of Sofia, the smell of trees and roses, the idleness of little squares. The strangest moment was at sunset. At that hour, when the sky was striped hard red and blue and the mountains violet and sharp beyond the pink roofs of the city, a din would break out of the church near the hotel. The little bells in the two cupolas would be rattled fast and the big bells would make a noise like cow bells; an irritable mixture of ding-dong and tin cans, as if some angry priest were trying to get the faithful to come and kiss the glass-protected picture-book images of countless saints. The glass of these pictures, I had noticed, was always covered with the clear imprint of scores of lips, so that the saint looked out at one through a cloud of ghostly mouths, some of which used lipstick.

The whole scene was more like a village scene than something in a city of fine buildings. My friends used to say: "They used to call this the cockpit of Europe, the hope of assassinations, wars, and massacres. It wasn't all our fault. You all muscled in on our politics—the Russians and Germans trying to get to the Bosporus, the British and French trying to stop them. We are peaceful now. We've reformed."

I hope we all have. My friend who translated Shelley said his one idea in life was not to take foreign writers around—not unless they liked country life as he did. Going up to the mountains, lazing in the sun, climbing, fishing, and sitting up half the night drinking gallons of wine and singing—being a real Bulgarian, he said, was his idea of happiness.

I was sad to fly off one evening to Romania.

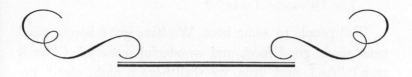

ROMANIA

Romania annoys from the beginning. With Czecho-slovakia it's the most rigid of the satellite states. The visitor is obliged to have a guide; the guide dogs your every step. He waits for you to come out of your bedroom in the morning. He bores you all day. He is informative, of course, but humourless, inclined to lecture, and is knowing. The relative freedom of Bulgaria has gone and, in any case, the Romanians despise the Bulgarians. I could not escape the impression that smooth hypocrisy and a reactionary state of mind are endemic. It is a large, rich country, afloat in oil.

In their moves towards contact with the West, each of the satellites has its own methods. The Romanians had decided at this time to open a night club in Bucharest.

"Tell people to come here. We have good hotels, good main roads, good food, and wonderful scenery." (This is true.) "And, next year, we shall have a night club," the officials say.

"That's a good idea," you say. "The Poles, the Czechs, the Hungarians, even the Bulgarians, have night clubs."

"Here, in Bucharest, no! But the policy has changed. We are going to have one. Just one," the officials say severely in the manner of people making discreet arrangements with sin on reformed lines, with guarantees.

Before the war Bucharest had been a city of pleasure and easy acquaintance. To the French it was a Ruritanian Paris in a hot climate, for the sedulous Romanians had created copies of the Champs-Elysées, the Arc de Triomphe, and a Bois de Boulogne with winding lakes that might have been the waterside of the Seine. There were deeply shaded avenues, there were boulevards, there were cafés in the open. There were innumerable clever Romanian writers, painters, sculptors, and musicians who had all been to Paris. Other nations had other views. The late Queen Mary, at a moment of crisis in the history of the British monarchy, clearly spoke of Romania as the synonym for deplorable scandal. The career of King Carol was a byword. Hungarians regarded Bucharest as a Montmartre blown up to city size, and Bulgarians crossed the frontier with the feeling that they were going to perdition. It seemed only too natural that the city should be the home of Dr. Voronoff and the monkey gland, and that notorious international septuagenarians should go there to have a grafting and renew their youth. Smooth, clever, sophisticated, masters in the art of assimilating foreign chic and culture, especially French, the Romanians made Europeans goggle at their intelligent pliancy. The Romanians claim to be the true descendants of the Romans. They have indeed the outward gravity of Latin peoples and they can certainly be said to have inherited the worldliness of the Roman decadence and the need to assimilate rather than to originate, though they produce good novelists and playwrights. And then the tie with France, which had lasted for more than a century, began to fail. France had taught revolutionaries and intellectuals ever since the days of Michelet; the intellectual life of Bucharest was French-formed and Italian-tinted. The hot-and-cold relationship with the Russians, who were on their northern frontier, became more intense: the attraction of Germany too powerful. Nazism in the form of the Iron Guard appeared. Anti-Semitism—always and still a powerful force in Romania—followed. When the war came, the Romanians, in whose racial mixture the Italianate-Slav predominates, changed sides towards the end of the fighting; the puritanical Russians, who had liberated them once before in their history, took over, and the light of the night clubs went out. The byword of Europe became the most conventional and rigid of the Communist states.

It still is. Unique among the satellites, Romania has known no real change in the Party leadership since the foundation of the regime. The "events" of 1956 in Hungary changed nothing; the Romanians kept a stern eye on their large Hungarian minority and this watchfulness alone was enough to prevent any liberalizing notions seeping in. The two countries, despite enthusiastic official visits, have a lot of past and temperamental differences to live down. Russian domination has, at any rate, kept the Balkans quiet. I always listen with special attention to the observations of foreign Communists about one another, and I have discovered only two main foreign opinions about Romania: (1) that the regime is severe and restrictive because of the racial diversity of the country and because of the long influence of the corruption of the past, and (2) the opposite view—that the regime is simply the Iron Guard under another name and a corrupt survival of Stalinism. Since 1961, it is said that the Russians have told the Romanians to relax, and one is told that this is happening. I did not notice it, but Bucharest is clearly cut out to be a city of talk and pleasure. For there is nothing grim on the surface of life in Romania; indeed it is all lazy, Latin, and engaging.

I was not in the country long enough to test thoroughly the accuracy of these remarks. I can only repeat that foreign Communists made them. Two political facts I can confidently record: that forced-labour camps still existed in Romania in 1960; that anti-Semitism is still strong. I know one Polish Communist who got into very serious high-level trouble in Warsaw for criticizing Romanian conditions in a Warsaw paper.

Against one's hostile impressions one has to put one or two remarkable achievements. The State has built and is running one of the largest and best printing works in Europe; it does a considerable amount of printing for the Soviet Union. The State also operates a huge new mass-production clothing and stocking factory equipped with the latest Czech and East German machinery. This factory clothes pretty well all Romania, and although most of the clothing is drab and without style, the better qualities are very presentable. This factory is like any modern Welfare corporation; it looks after every detail of the lives of its thousands of employees from cradle to grave. While the machines knit the stockings and the knives slice out dozens of coats, jackets, and pairs of trousers at a blow, the children of the workers are being looked after in cheerful creches, schools, and playgrounds. The children are prettily dressed. There are photographs of the old factory on this site to show what progress has been made; and in these old pictures it is repellent to see the workers filing up to get their pay from overseers, who wear uniforms, under the eyes of armed police. At least *that* has gone. The disadvantages of life in this modern beehive, with its concert halls, hospitals, and canteens, is that there is theoretical but not real freedom to leave it for another job. To change is possible, but difficult. Obviously for those who like mass life or have no other choice, this place is good.

One is continually told that the State has developed other things which had been neglected; that the oil fields, for example, have been brought up to date. The shops in the Callea Victoriei, once the Rue de la Paix of Bucharest, must be far below the old standard, for there are no rich or even moderately well-off people to buy anything; but the shopwindows are dressed with a good deal of art, and are more attractive to look at than the windows of Prague. There was an exhibition of consumer goods going on, and the tweeds and textiles were attractive; the tinned foods, wines, and cheeses were excellent, and the exhibition was arranged with taste and was packed out by well-dressed people. My guide was proud to point out the displays of optical instruments—a new industry, he said. Handicrafts, always very important in this country, thrive and are more attractive here than elsewhere in Eastern Europe.

I drove a hundred miles from Bucharest into the Carpathians. The mountain resorts have excellent modern hotels. One eats delicious food, drinks good wine. One is astonished by the beauty of the women, which comes from the lucky mixture of Mediterranean and Slavonic types: the dark-haired, white-skinned Italian women, the full, fair-haired, and blue-eyed Slavonic girls who have lost the hardness of the Slav and are soft and southern. Romania has the southern ease and, I have no doubt, the profound southern respect for custom. Two small and contrasting incidents stick in my mind. The Romanians have not driven off the beggars. I saw many in Bucharest. Some bent or ragged old woman or man would come into one of those hot, cushioned cafés in the Boulevard N. Bălcescu and murmur at every table. In the old tradition of Latin charity, every customer went to some trouble to dig a note or a coin out of his pocket for them. The beggars were never refused; nor did they harry, whine, or explain. Both parties knew their immemorial roles, and with lazy impersonality stuck to the ritual. Romanian Communism is an improvement on Franco's Fascism in this respect; unlike the Spaniards, the Romanians have not carted the beggars out of the capitals so that visitors shall not see them.

But where there is lazy convention, there is also bound to be tyranny. The other incident is not flattering to the

Romanian state in its present obdurate frame of mind. When I was leaving Bucharest, my bag was, of course, opened by the Customs. On top of my things was a letter I had received from my wife. The Customs officer pounced on it.

"What is this?" he said. "You can't take this out of the country."

"Why not?"

"It is forbidden to take correspondence abroad."

My guide helped me out, and the officer shrugged his shoulders dubiously and let the matter go.

"You see," Apollo said (my guide was called Apollo), "he thought *you* had written the letter. Some Romanians try to get their letters posted abroad, in order to save money on the postage. It is cheating the post office, and we have to stop it."

This farcical lie was blandly spoken. When I said the motive was obviously political, he swore that it was not. Apollo had always been bland and impenetrable. What he discreetly did not tell me was that letters sent abroad have to be taken personally by the writer to the post office and handed in—at any rate until recently—unsealed. I shall have more to say about my guides in Bucharest.

I did not intend to have a guide there. The difficulties of the language itself are not so severe as they are, say, in Bulgaria or Hungary. For Romanian is a Latin tongue and to anyone who knows Spanish or Italian a certain amount gets through. In any case, large numbers of people speak French—I found, for example, French-speaking shoeblacks. But a guide was waiting for me at the airport with a large car and a program. I gave in. My first guide was a fair, patient, severe young man of twenty-six, more Slav than Italian. His name was Iozu.

The sky was soft blue, the air sweet and lazy. At midday at the end of November, it was hot. The soft heat came in dusty lungfuls out of the side streets and down the boulevards. One walked under trees. Little chrysanthemums were planted round each one. The vermilion trams, narrow and German-looking, went fast down the boulevard, where motor traffic is light. One had the impression here that one was on a film set or in the middle of exhibition architecture that had not lasted. This may be because Bucharest was severely damaged during the war—the R.A.F. not only had concentrated on the oil wells at Ploeşti, but also had bombarded the city; one bomb destroyed the opera house—but the fact is that a lot of the high blocks of flats and offices were put up in the racketeering period between the wars in the fever to be "modern" too quick. It was a period of poor workmanship and gloss; now the plaster has dropped off the façades, yards at a time; shutters had jammed or rusted; no paint had been put on for years. The older buildings of Bucharest are in a much better state than those put up in this period; and the new buildings going up now look very good. I minded official architecture much less here than in any of the other Communist countries; the Romanians have the Italian sense of style, show, and placing and the Italian feeling for life on the surface. Bucharest was celebrating its 500th anniversary that year, and so the stress on building, on encouraging the Romanian styles, and on cleaning up was very strong. There has always been a marked feeling in the country for folk and regional things—no question here of the artificial encouragement of handicrafts; they have always been very important in the life and the economy—and there were a number of open-air, patio-type cafés with thatched loggias in the main boulevards which added to the air of exhibition. The thing to do at this time of year in these cafés was to drink *must*, the new season's juice of the grape. You drink it out of a heavy painted mug, and you eat perhaps one of those large peppers that look like hard tomatoes and set the mouth on fire; or pickled cucumbers or sausage or some savoury Greek mess done up in vine leaves. While people in the North of Europe are shivering in late November, in Bucharest you can still sit out in the evenings, and the only winter sign is the sight of hot doughnuts being ladled out of their tanks of syrup from stalls or windows in the streets. My second guide, Apollo, was not very keen on sitting around drinking *must*. He preferred standing at the chest-high tables of the modern espressos because it was easier to fall into conversation with girls—but my first day was not Apollo's; it was Iozu's, and Iozu's mind was bent on politics. He was a dour young man with an ulcered stomach who was going to join the Party next year.

We went off to the older parts of the flat city. Bucharest lies on the grain-bearing plain, which, in the nineteenth century, had been third among the grain-bearing places of the world, before the Argentine and the United States had vastly surpassed it. Five hundred years ago, the city began around the inns attached to one or two Orthodox monasteries, and it has spread out very much like a traveller's encampment or a rich and crowded market ever since. There must have been money in Bucharest at one time; it must have been a dealer's, speculator's city, enlarged by feudal fortunes. The oil industry must have brought great wealth to it. It retains the air of a bazaar where rich and poor jostle along together; the steady middle-class appearance of Prague, a middle class disguised in proletarian clothes, is something clearly alien to Bucharest, and, in consequence, the sights and contrasts of the street are more interesting. Not only that—the Romanians exhibit themselves well. There was a very fine historical exhibition which really did give a vivid notion of the city's growth stage by stage; the social-political side of it showed a far keener sense of history than I had expected. It was not unbearably tendentious. The photographs and relics of the important pre-war rising, strikes, riots, and repressions were admirably done. They brought home the fact which the tourist is apt to forget, as he also does in Spain, that picturesque peasant life had its terrible side—there was a peasant rising in 1907—and that life for the industrial worker in a country that had not outgrown the feudal ethos was hell.

The liveliest part of Bucharest is down by the market. Here the famous Gypsy flower sellers sit, long rows of stalwarts behind their great baskets of flowers. They were one of the vivid splashes of colour in the place; on the opposite side of the street is the confusion of the fruit and vegetable stalls. Thousands swarm among them. A good deal of private trade survives here. The peasants, with their high-crowned fleece hats, the women in their coloured scarves, fight their way into the melee. The life of the market-bazaar is far from having vanished in this city. At seven or eight in the evening the celebrated Lipscana Street —so called because it sells what are called Leipzig goods, mainly clothing—is so packed with people that one can hardly walk down it. All the cities of southern Europe have the habit of living outside in dense crowds.

It was the day of St. Demetrius, an important day for Bucharest and the Orthodox Church. We climbed the long hill from the flower market in the Piata to the great ugly church where the Patriarch would be chanting. Iozu, who was going to join the Party next year, was torn in two by the feast. He was fervent for the local customs of his city; he was pleased to be able to boast that the Orthodox Church had never been a stumbling block to the Party and that it had never become involved obstructively in politics in the manner of the Roman Catholic Church. The Orthodox appears to be a less rigid confession. Its priests can marry; they can be divorced. It has been simple to deal with the Orthodox Church because it had lost most of its income from its once large estates in the land reforms before the war; and it was easy for Iozu to admire the Patriarch because he co-operates with the Party. And although the Party reorganized the Church when it came to power, the new organization closely resembled the old. The Party has recognized that the huge peasant population of Romania is solidly pious and that they will be slow to budge from their beliefs.

And so it appeared, for from early morning to late at night an unending procession of thousands of people, mainly women, filed patiently up the hill to the basilica. The procession never stopped. Contrary to Iozu's argument, the people looked middle-class. Each person carried a small bottle in which he would collect a year's supply of holy water at the fountain outside the church. In the coming year they would sprinkle a drop or two upon themselves, on their families, animals, things—on anything which involved the fulfilling of a wish: a drop or two on a sick person to make them better, on a wife or a husband to make them do something or other, on the house to make it lucky. Some were carrying pieces of paper on which a written request is made and presented to the priest.

Iozu said: "It may seem to you indelicate, but I have once or twice peeped over someone's shoulder to read what was written. One I read said: 'Please see that So-and-So is struck dead; she has gone off with my husband.' And quite a lot say outright: 'Get So-and-So out of the flat in such-and-such a street, so that I can have it.' "

Whether he really read this or not, I am sure that Romanian wishes are passionate and cunning. Romania is the country of the vampire legend.

While we were talking, the superb voice of the Patriarch in the Greek chant came out of the microphone in the trees outside the church—a voice powerful, disturbing, sensual, and full. It was a life-giving rather than a censorious nasal sound—the note I have always found tyrannous in the Roman rite. Iozu said that the Patriarch was very popular and was known by the nickname of "the-too-happy." His earthly and assuring noise was followed by the wild, utterly Oriental tenor howl of the Deacon, who might have been whining in the desert or screaming a *saeta* in Seville. The two voices played upon each other, and their spell was wonderful. And while they chanted, the mile-long procession slowly crept into the church and those who came out went around to kiss the walls. It was a hot morning, and this is a kissing religion—walls, stones, fountains, innumerable pictures of saints to be kissed. The lip prints are thick on them.

Iozu took me to the new football stadium to show me that Romanians were modern as well as medieval. We saw the new building estates, not very impressive; the gardens were burned up by the sun and neglected. We were driving through a city of trees, for one craves for shade in the autumn as well as the summer. Old Bucharest has a distinctive architectural style—the single-storey house with heavy overhanging eaves and carved porch; many took my mind back to old Lima and Portugal. The dahlias, the roses, the chrysanthemums and michaelmas daisies were flopping in the gardens. Iozu talked about his life. He was a boy when the war ended, the son of a factory worker. There was confusion when the Romanians changed sides and joined the British and the Russians. The British were not popular because they had bombed the oil fields and the city continually, and Iozu said all the young boys ran wild. He spent wonderful days pulling down polling booths, and the British arrested his father and mother. Iozu then joined the Communist Pioneers and quickly got a good education. He spoke English, French, German, and Russian, and he had been sent as an interpreter to Scandinavia, Russia, and Italy. He was not impressed. He was keen on joining the Party, and when I carelessly said: "It would be to your advantage," he was indignant. One got no "advantages" from the Party. One was generally worse paid than anyone else. But one learned to be a leader who would guide people out of the morass of backwardness and superstition. He had a very clear idea of the distinction between real leaders, exhibitionists, and careerists. He said all Romanians, like himself, were utterly out of sympathy with the Hungarian rising, chiefly (he admitted) for nationalist reasons. Once again, the strongest feeling in all the satellites, except Czechoslovakia, is national. I never saw Iozu smile. He was a Slav, fair, blue-eyed, crop-headed, and severe. He tried hard to do his duty and find out everything I did in Bucharest. He nearly went mad when he lost me in the food exhibition.

Iozu left me; he had to conduct a busload of Czechs to Budapest. One could tell the difference between the Czech and the Russian busloads in the dining room of the hotel. The Czech parties were terribly shapeless and ugly and badly dressed; the Russians were stolid, and the material of their clothes was very thin and poor. They drank no beer or wine, and they waited and waited, until at last the busy, cynical waiters rushed great platters of fried pork chops and chips to them.

My second guide was Apollo. There was nothing of the incipient Party member about Apollo. Dark, handsome in the Italian style, he was always hanging about the girls in the hotel. He knew everybody and was always late. He was the only son of a retired doctor whose wife added to their small pension by teaching history in a secondary school. They sent him money. He had been to Russia and had

been a success with the girls there. "They always fall for
the southern type," he said unsmilingly. "Russian men are
not interesting to them." In the meantime, Apollo was
thinking of getting married to a girl in Bucharest. Their
official jobs had given them both pull; and they were lucky
to have a two-room flat each. "That is what is holding up
our marriage," he said. "She won't give up her flat and I
don't want to give up mine. And then I'm so busy with
foreign visitors all summer and autumn that I don't get
time to see much of her till the winter. That is the time for
love—the winter, when things are quiet and you can stay
inside. It's too cold to go out, anyway. And then, of course,
I may get a job in foreign trade. I want to go on trade
delegations to the West. What do you think of that blonde?
She's in the airline office."

"She's very pretty," I said.

"Hi, sweet," called Apollo to the girl. "This gentleman
says he adores you."

The girl shrugged and went off.

"I know so many," Apollo said.

Apollo spoke no English. His French was excellent. He
had never been to France.

One got bored by taking foreigners round the Pioneer
school, the print works, the clothing factory, he said, and
foreigners were funny. The British didn't want to see
much, but wanted to go into one or two things deeply.
They were dull. The Americans wanted to go everywhere
and talked of nothing but dollars, and their women got
drunk on whiskey. The Germans were rude. The worst
were the French. They were fantastically mean. They

astonished the waiters by asking them to save their table napkins for the next meal and to keep the unfinished bottles of wine for them. The waiters rushed to the kitchens and shouted with laughter. "No one drinks less than a whole bottle of wine in Romania," he said. Apollo lectured me on the excellence of everything in Communist Romania; he was wonderfully conceited, efficient, and incapable of discussion. For example, one day I asked him what would happen if he overdrew his account at the bank. He said he had no bank account. He had never heard of cheque books. He said there were no private bank accounts, and all savings had been confiscated when the Communists took over. He said he was paid in cash and kept his money in a drawer at home.

"Aren't you afraid it might be stolen?"

"There are no thieves in Romania," he said. "Under Communism there is no stealing, no burglary, no gangster life, as there is in the West. There would be no point in it. Look," he said, picking up a newspaper. "There are no reports of crime."

"Perhaps they are suppressed for political reasons."

"There is no crime, but if there were, to publish reports would only encourage the criminals and make the public morbid," he said. If he saved money, he put it in the savings bank. Apollo was superficially well educated. He was intelligent about the very fine Grecos in the Royal Palace, now the National Gallery. He told me about books, and he was good on modern literature and proud of the tradition of Romanian folk tales. He knew his country thoroughly and did his job perfectly. We went one night to hear *Don*

Pasquale—to our disappointment we could not get into the Grand Opera House—and he was displeased because he had shown me a poor performance. In music Bucharest has high standards.

Bucharest has a peculiar distinction among the world's capitals. The Romanians enjoy a Methuselah complex. They desire to live forever. They loathe old age. For fifty years they have had the handsomely endowed Parhon Institute for Geriatrics. At present it is run by a remarkable woman doctor, Dr. Aslan, whose researches are well known in Europe and the United States. She is a busy and most engaging woman who looks a young forty—but, as she proudly says, is much older—who works sixteen hours a day, loves conversation and showing off her extraordinary troupe of old men and women, whose infirmities she has cured and who enjoy a surprising rejuvenation. They march into her office headed by the celebrated Parseh Margosian, aged 112, a man with a hand grip of iron, a commanding eye, a neck as smooth as a baby's, new-grown hair on his rugged head. Once in a state of physical and mental decay, he can now chatter in the seven Eastern languages he was brought up in, and strides about manfully. There is a lively tailor who has returned to his trade at 76, after paralysis; he is now growing black hair. One frightening fellow of 80, a onetime gymnasium instructor, did a handstand on the table beside me. Another ancient has lately married a young thing in her sixties and reproaches her only for having passed the age of childbearing and so has failed, in Congreve's phrase, to crown their endeavours. A lady in her seventies, an opera singer who had lost her voice and become a physical wreck, sang an aria at the top of her voice and was asked not to go "all out." I came away with a mangled hand—the hand grip is the vanity of great age. Apollo was with me. Dr. Aslan told him old age begins when you are born and that injections of procaine would do him good. Giving me a sharp look, she said I would recover an optimistic outlook on life and improve my memory. One feels younger after listening to Dr. Aslan. Perhaps she is a splendid Romanian sorceress, reborn in science.

Apollo told me he had ampules of procaine in his flat and was waiting for the first signs of failing powers. Perhaps next year. . . . Perhaps before the next trip to Russia. . . . He would be twenty-six, a critical age. The clinic is a mixture of laboratory, hospital, and old folks' home. The old people have charming rooms and sit about reading to each other or listening to the wireless. It reminded me of a fine home for the aged I had seen in Connecticut.

The Carpati organization—the State tourist agency—who are anxious to get people from the West to go to Romania, and do in fact get a number of German, French, and American tourists, told Apollo to take me to Orăşul-Stalin (late Braşov) up in the southern Carpathians, here called the Transylvanian Alps. If I had had time I would have gone farther north, to the Lacul Roşu, with its strange lake on which one sails over the treetops of a petrified forest, and then westward to towns like Cluj and Oradea. The mountain and forest scenery was upholstered in greenery. Before leaving Bucharest, I had visited the remarkable outdoor museum called The Romanian Village (an enterprise already flourishing before the Second World War), because here, close to the lake, are examples of peasant house-building from all the regions of Transylvania. Essentially the Romanians are decorators. There is something Oriental in the architecture of their houses and the decorative taste appears in carving, in their murals, in the wooden-slatted roofs of their farm buildings and cottages, and in the high wooden steeples of their churches, which shoot up like the long necks of storks with wings outspread over the nest.

Hour after hour we drove under the yellow acacias northwards from Bucharest across the flat Romanian Plain. For miles the road was lined by whitewashed wooden fences, and behind them were occasional settlements of wooden cabins. It was peasant country. Scores of little carts loaded with wood, bricks, rushes, or sacks of potatoes were being drawn by ponies. The peasant families sat on top of the load, the men in their fez-like hats of brown sheepskin, the women in their head scarves. Industrial workers around Ploeşti, where the oil fields are, have given up the sheepskin hat and are taking to cloth caps and berets. Apollo quickly pointed out the modern derricks that had replaced the old ones in the oil fields. They add an iron melancholy to the flat landscape of pale burned grasses. Ploeşti itself was badly bombed in the war, and is a shabby, crowded town. Now the road began to rise into the mountains, and we drove above the pretty Prahova River, passing the mountain sawmills, the cement works, the paper mills in the gorges, and then into the wilder, fir-forested heights. Little towns of holiday villas appeared, and higher up were brilliant patches of Alpine pasture. The things that caught my eye continually were the almost mosque-like villas. One was in the heart of Romania. Up here was the fantastic Hohenzollern castle, an appalling pile of nineteenth-century rococo in the worst German taste. The pomp, the excreted extravagance of chocolate-coloured wood carving in this gloomy pseudo-fortress is worth looking at. It tells one everything about Germanic royalty in the nineteenth century—its congested arrogance, its comic medievalism, its ludicrous pomp, half martial, half sickly, fanciful, and childish. One is shown the little desk at which the Prime Minister had to stand as he waited for the seated King to sign the documents. All one can say is that they had a superb eagle's view of the Carpathian peaks as they dipped their pens. How any human being walked about in safety is a wonder, for the floors of the palace are like glass. We were given slippers and, with a couple of pretty French-speaking girls who were our guides, we slid about, giggling.

"What can one do with a place like this?" they said, skating hilariously down the corridors in their flannel slippers. "It is hopeless as a retreat for writers, a library, a rest house for workers. Perhaps we ought to have a psychiatrists' conference here, to discuss suicide and nightmares."

Charabanc-loads of people from Bucharest come up to gape and laugh at the monstrosity and to ramble up the mountain paths.

Like all historic monuments in the country, this is impeccably well kept.

Orăşul-Stalin is made up of an old medieval town and a modern industrial one in the tractor-and-lorry-building trade. The industry was set up by the Germans during the war; since then the Romanians have enlarged it and built a worker's community near it. The whole mountain region is a place of hotels, and Orăşul-Stalin has the parklike attraction of a nineteenth-century spa. Here the Carpathians are tamed; the hunting grounds where, if you are lucky, you see the bear, the roebuck, and the wolves are further north, where one approaches the Ukraine. Rich West Germans hunt there still.

There is a luxury hotel at Orăşul-Stalin, where one dines well to the noise of a jazz band, and people dance, but it was almost empty when we were there. We had more amusement round the corner in the crowded cafeteria, where a cheerful crowd were eating delicious food and drinking their *slivovitz* and *zwiecke*, a neat, plum spirit that smells and tastes like Dettol; even better, there was one of those cellar cafés which are common in the region, packed out with workers who eat and drink generously. Winters are hard here; for nearly half the year northeast winds come fiercely down from Russia, and people dive underground into these clean, light places, which are warmed by the lovely tiled stoves of the country. They stand like ornate private shrines in the rooms. Pretty well the whole of Romania is heated by natural gas that is piped down from the mountains. I have often complained of the defects of service in the cafés, bars, and hotels of Eastern Europe; in Romania, one cannot make this criticism. In the smart places or in the popular ones, like these hot cellar cafés, the attention is quick and cheerful. Tips were always refused. Conversation roared in the cellar. Apollo amused himself

135

by picking out the Hungarians, who are a majority in this region; we talked about mural paintings in the village churches, the wonders of natural gas, the general prosperity of Romania. We wandered about the gay crowded streets until the night fogs came down. The chauffeur had supper with us, but as he did not speak French, I got nothing out of him. Even Apollo complained that he would not talk. For days he had been a silent man, worrying about his batteries.

I had arrived in Romania from Bulgaria. One flies over the Balkans and then over the sad fens and puddled lagoons of the Danube. The little plane was a day late; it was grounded in Sofia—all planes were grounded, because Khrushchev was flying back to Moscow after a secret visit to Bucharest. Foreign diplomats discovered he had been there for a week only when they opened their newspapers the day after he left. Apollo told me it was easy for politicians to get in and out of the city without being observed, for they live out by the lake which adjoins the airport. An official need never go into the heart of the capital. After poor, primitive, energetic Bulgaria, I was struck by the sophistication and comparative wealth of the Romanians. I was once more in a country nearer to Western Europe, although, like Bulgaria, it had lived for three hundred years under the overlordship of the Turks. But the Turks had oppressed the Romanians less; they had ruled through the Romanian boyars or small nobility. After the First World War, Romania became immensely enlarged and even oversized at Hungarian expense, which has left serious minority problems. Romanians are by tradition authoritarian and harsh rulers. I visited a royal palace which has been turned into a special and delightfully housed school for favoured pupils, the Pioneers, who have lovely grounds to wander in, and I was struck by the stern little boys who policed—it is the only word—the corridors of the school. Heels clicked. Salutes. The display of children's work was quite good—with the startling exception of the drawing and painting. The imaginative painting of children, which has been a revelation in the last thirty years in the West, is quite unknown. The carving, on the other hand, was excellent: it is a Romanian skill. At their cinema, the children were looking at the usual war film about the Partisans. Apollo thought it all splendid. I'm afraid only the situation and the prettiness of the children impressed me.

Now Romania has over seventeen million people. It is hard to know what progress they were making. They had a period of great prosperity between the wars which put them on their feet. Have they improved or gone back? There is little in the way of reliable information to guide one. The diplomatic gossip is that the regime is "losing its grip"—whatever that may mean. At any rate, the Romanians were building fast; I saw no signs of shortages in basic things—certainly there was not the sort of food shortage you get in Poland. The head of the cultural organization was bland. "We always produce an enormous number of poets," he said, "but not exceptionally good ones." They have one or two good novelists and here—this is exceptional in Eastern Europe—one or two of the best ones firmly support the Party without *arrière pensée*. A quick, sedate, acquisitive, rather pompous intelligence is noticeable everywhere—an open mistrust of Western foreigners, too. I heard an American lady explaining about her alimony to a young Romanian interpreter, a pleasant girl who might have come out of Radcliffe or Somerville. "We do not allow alimony here," the girl said sternly. "Only an allowance for children. Women here prefer to work. There are no idle divorcees." The women are very conscious of being better to look at and better dressed than their Russian visitors. Apollo, continually hopping off to check up on something—perhaps to report on me, more probably to see what new girls had turned up—with his eye on the future, his hopeful contacts, the cosy flat he had got from a friend, clearly kept in with the good things of life.

"Now," he said to me in a bored, sarcastic voice as I got on the international plane, "now you will be able to read your Western papers."

One more boring Western visitor was going. Dutiful to the end, he stayed and waved and waved. He even smiled. He had a blonde with him, a real beauty.

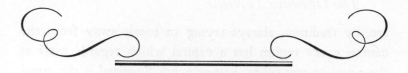

MADRID

Madrid is the invented capital. It is an idea in red brick, iron-grey stone, and flashing concrete, rising in the middle of the Castilian steppe. Until twenty-five years ago it was low and almost invisible from the plain; now it is ringed by high, upended white rectangular blocks and can at last be seen. In 1560 it was a scheme in the mind of Philip II, who turned a half-Arab village into a capital.

In the main street of the working-class quarter called Cuatro Caminos, on the northern outskirts of the city, there is a small shop with the name El Ciento Siete, 107. On its door the proprietor, indignant with the local government officials, has put the true number in large figures: 109. Always growing, always anomalous, Madrid is never quite sure of its identity. For Spain is a collection of regions that are, by tradition, always trying to break away from the centre; every region has a capital which regards itself as the equal of any other, just as every Spaniard is the equal of every other Spaniard. Philip II, the subtle centralizer of the sixteenth century, determined to keep every detail of the management of the largest empire since the Roman in his own hands, and so invented a small capital. He desired a small place where he could work without interruption, while the deeper solitude of the monastery of El Escorial, twenty-five miles away in the Guadarrama Mountains, was being prepared for him. The new capital recognized its artificiality. Madrid is rarely called the capital; even today it dislikes calling itself a city—the word is too commonplace and impersonal. It is known, with negligent family pretension, as the Villa or the Corte.

By the rest of Spain, Madrid is also called the parasite. Tourists who travel too fast and who look for the standard Spanish clichés think the city dull. Once they have seen the Prado, the Royal Palace, and the seventeenth-century Plaza Mayor and have looked for antiques in the Rastro or flea market, they move quickly on. For them it is a comfortable centre from which to visit more interesting places. Yet Madrid is one of the most livable cities in Europe for those who believe in the untroublesome pleasures of life. With its shaded boulevards, its Metro, it is something of an imitation Paris shut off from Western Europe by Spanish stubbornness, but it is not electric, it is not perfumed, it is not feminine, intellectual, or modish.

It is a male city, run for lazy men and the slack masculine kindness: even the women have something of the male in their harsh voices and their sharp looks. One would say that this is a place to which the men have brought all their relations to live and have then got out of their houses to avoid them. Hence, a glum and footloose air about the crowds; no one wants to go home—he knows what he'll find there! There is no chic. The romantic Napoleonic Madrid of Goya, the Madrid of the *majo y maja,* of the picnics at San Isidro, of the yellow and gold silks and the shawls of Manila, went a long time ago, and in Madrid much depended on such things. At a first night in the theatre, one sees occasionally an odd gentleman wearing a black cloak with the crimson lining, muffling his face as he goes out into the cruel air of the Madrid winter. And women going to Mass or confession, to a wedding or a funeral, will cobweb themselves in the black mantilla. These are survivals. The Madrid crowd of today, overwhelmingly lower-middle-class, has joined what the Madrileños call the cheap-gabardine civilization.

So one does not go to Madrid for the sights. The deep attraction of Madrid is in its people, their liveliness and manners. Yet, before we speak of them, let us mention the city's most important physical distinction; it is pretty well the highest capital in Europe. It stands on the tableland over 2,000 feet above sea level, in air that is dry and fluttering. The Castilian wind is continuously flickering under the nostrils, a wind that is kind in spring and grateful in the summer, but deadly to the weak-chested on winter nights, when it is glacial and blows over the wet or the snowy stone. It is the proverbial wind that will not blow out a candle but will kill a man.

141

But against the wind we have to put the light. Outside of Greece there is no light to compare with the Spanish, especially the light of Castile: Madrid is less the capital of Spain than the capital of the Castilian light. In the hot months it is pure fire, refined to the incandescence of a furnace, and it is like the gleam of armour in the cold winter. It is so limpid that you feel you have only to reach out to run your fingers over the peaks of the Sierra in the distance. At sunset, the buildings, the helmet spires of churches, cut the hard green sky; it is the armed military moment of the Spanish cities. By day the light has the radiance of enamel. It is rare to see a cloud in the sky above Madrid after March and before November, and if one small puff of cloud does sail over, people stop in the street and look at it as if it were something lost.

The effect of such a light, without mists and without soft shadows, is to remove illusion; everything stares in its detail, as if every leaf or brick or rock were crowded with impersonal eyes. We see the same stare in the details of the clothes worn by Spanish kings in the pictures of Velázquez. In this light the painter learned his realism, as perhaps Goya learned his in the fire of the Madrid noon, and El Greco sought his colours in the hard, bruised dunes between Madrid and Toledo.

Twenty-five years ago the first sight one had of Madrid was the long white flush of the eighteenth-century Royal Palace on its cliff above the Manzanares, that poor dried-up river now turned into a concrete canal. The Palace led one to expect a sumptuous city, but no other building in the capital approached its magnificence. Madrid, the people

said with affection, was no more than a pueblo, a town. It
had one or two minor palaces, but they were dull. It had a
population of 800,000.

The once horizontal city has become vertical; it sticks
up into the light and the wind. Eighteen years after the
Civil War, it doubled its population; it will soon have
2,000,000. The place which once stopped dead in the
ploughed land at the end of the Castellana—the little
Champs-Elysées of Madrid—has spread chaotically into the
sandy building lots and arterial roads of the steppe. The
peasants from the poor southern provinces have left their villages en masse and have come to the capital. They are working for the builders who are responding to the dictator's
appetite for monuments, skyscrapers, colleges, convents,
churches, and immense buildings for the new civil service
of the syndicalist state. Madrid has lost its identity and has
become foreign to its inhabitants. Some look at the new city
with pride, some with mistrust—for how can a poor country
afford it? All are dumfounded. Suddenly and very late,
Madrid has left the nineteenth century and joined the
twentieth.

The fact is that the city has moved out of the economy
of small commerce and into the modern world of finance
capitalism. It is being built and occupied by the tough
corporations of the Basque bankers. It is even being industrialized. Sadly, people say, "Madrid is beginning to work."

For centuries the city had produced nothing very much.
That character remains in spirit, if it is changing in fact.
From the time of the Empire, Madrid has lived for the
ease of office, for pleasure, and for spoils. The houses were

often austerely furnished. The family fortune in all classes was spent on public show, on social life or personal display in the streets.

A city of the servants of servants of servants, Madrid is now ruled, family fashion, by a general and his near relations who manipulate the three powerful forces in the country: the Church, the army, and the Falange or neo-Fascist party. One has the impression of stepping into family life. The Madrileño is a man of attachments and friendships. His pleasures are small and are the things that give him no trouble: sitting, strolling, staring, sleeping, talking. He ignores the clock. Life in Madrid is not lived at a high, nervous pitch. People are themselves. More conventional than the Frenchman, less naïve than the Italian, the Madrileño is a natural observer, sceptical and realistic. But fundamentally he regards himself as "formal," even Victorian; he admires the distinguished—the *distinguido*. He is quick to perceive and answer and anticipate. He is abstemious in drink, extravagant in opinion, violent when moved. If at first sight he appears glum, this is merely because he is waiting to be lit up and to crackle into life and frivolity. For his malicious wit, he is famous. There is probably a larger daily output of political epigram in Madrid than in any other capital on earth. The habit of living under a dictatorship encourages the cynicism. "To the Pope's intentions," says the young novelist in trouble with the ecclesiastical censorship, raising his glass.

The Madrileño will sacrifice comfort, property, everything, to the public appearance. The sacred hour of the *paseo* at six in the evening, when the women come out and the crowd walk up and down the street, is the time of dis-

play. The cinema and the theatre crowds are elegant. The
people do not slump into pleasure. Pleasure is an occasion.
Nothing shocks the Madrileño so much as the foreign
tourists' indifference to their appearance. Northerners, to
him, are vulgar in their dress and their activity. In his heart
he agrees with the hungry poor knight in the most famous
of the picaresque novels, *Lazarillo de Tormes*, that it can
be more important to appear to have eaten than to be able
to eat.

There are three Madrids: the city of the dry, hard,
splendacious twentieth century; the Villa or Corte of the
nineteenth, the place of old boulevards, balconies, small
rattling elevators with gates that catch the knuckles, enormous brass-studded or carved doors, high unheated rooms
and dark, windowless alcoves for bedrooms; and the old
Madrid of convents, alleys, markets, and the outlying
wagoners' inns.

The twentieth-century city looks South American. It
has not yet enough electricity to go round. In the last few
years the sky signs of the Gran Via have gone out and the
restaurants have been lit by pressure lamps until the cur-
rent is switched on again. You can see the struggle between
the nineteenth and twentieth centuries in the trams. The old
grinding cars are being replaced by swift modern ones and
by trolley buses. There are even a few old ill-treated
London buses, painted blue. Madrid traffic, which used to
be stuck fast for hours in the evening, now moves. But in
the older parts of the city you can still see at night one
of the red or blue trams waiting, say, at Santo Domingo like
a battered Chinese lantern.

Nineteenth-century Madrid has the shade of trees, the

145

bourgeois decorum; also a narrow, genteel anxiety to conceal anxiety about money. A large number of middle-class men are feverishly looking for ways of picking up commissions here and there. In a neighbourhood like the Puerta del Sol and the hilly streets around it, shabbiness has come in. The famous square where the populace comes out on New Year's Eve, to eat twelve grapes as the clock strikes twelve, is going downhill. The old cafés are going. But there are still, on the first floors, the celebrated barbershops which are the male gossip clubs. As one moves toward the Royal Palace into the formal garden of the Plaza de Oriente and the Plaza Isabel Segunda, there is quiet and there is propriety. From the Palace back to the Castellana, to the deep-shaded walks of the Retiro, at whose gates every Sunday the servant girls meet or exchange their young men as if it were an open-air marriage market; to the rose walls and cedar trees of the Prado—all this has the graciousness of an older age.

When the traveller visits the Royal Palace, he is taken round in a small party, perhaps of people from some provincial town, by one of the old long-coated servants who will speak of how they waited at King Alfonso's table. There are Goyas mocking Carlos IV and Maria Luisa. There is the throne room with its golden chair, where General Franco receives ambassadors; the beautiful rooms done in the lovely porcelain of the Retiro factory which Napoleon destroyed. There is a firmament of chandeliers—and to the Spaniard, the chandelier is the symbol of success. "So-and-So has arrived," they say. "He has got his chandelier."

146

"It puzzles me that people go to the cinema," the servant says disdainfully to the crowd, "when they could come here and see far greater luxury."

"But we do not live in Madrid," the provincial protests.

"A pity," says the servant, and walks away to announce a new treasure. "*Sí, señor,*" he says long afterwards, as an afterthought. It has a formal ecclesiastical tone. He is saying "Amen."

These heavy-coated servants of Madrid, tall and am-bassadorial, guarding the great doors, reborn for the doors of apartment houses and cinema and night-club entrances, are a special race of men. They are as poor as they are magnificent; and if one of them gives a final spit from a doorway across the pavement into the street before he turns in at night, the act has all that is grand and cere-monious and familiar in the Spanish temper. They speak in proverbs. "It is a cold night," you say as you go into the warm house. "But for those who have the peseta it is warm," is the reply. "*Sí, señor.*" Amen. So God intended it.

The Madrileño makes all things familiar. The Palace yard with its fine view across the plain makes a sun trap for the nurses, the mothers, the black-shawled women knitting and sewing on their stools while hundreds of children play around them. In sun or shade, according to the season, the families take over the doorsteps, the pave-ments, the spaces, the city.

Many of the great houses are now museums, but the Duke of Alba's palace is still a private home. It was burnt to the ground in the Civil War, and has now been rebuilt. Its library is almost gone, but most of the best pictures were saved, including a number of Goyas. Galdós and Goya still rule the older spirit of the city; and it was indeed in a spirit primitive and Goyesque that the palace was burnt down in the Civil War. Its gardens are still haunted by horrors. There was a giant, brutal man who appointed himself to take charge of the ruin before the city fell and who used to go out at night sniping like a hunter, bringing back his victims slung on his shoulders, like shot rabbits. He buried them reverently in the palace gardens. That was, as the Madrileño says, something *muy español*, inexplicable, savage: the mixture of the primitive and some obscure act of courtesy like the last cigarette offered at an execution.

A milder example of the *muy español* is the curious home of the Marqués de Cerralbo. The Marqués was an indiscriminate collector, and his house is an absurd jumble of nineteenth-century taste. The artist who painted the ceilings was sacked because he painted nymphs in the nude, for the Spanish taste has a marked puritan strain. This house is drenched in golden luxury, but it is all for display. There was something of the hermit in its owner. His bedroom is as bleak as a monk's cell and hung with gloomy religious images. There is so often an ascetic and frugal core inside the Spanish voluptuary. In the great houses, with their tapestries, in the modern houses of the moderately well off, we have the sensation that a people who are gay in public like to preserve the sense of life as a private sadness. The same people who shout in each other's faces when roused go back to glum, uncomfortable, solitary meditation afterward.

148

There is also a tendency toward the life of single purpose. The Madrileño who works half kills himself with two or three jobs. He is at the government office in the morning, at a business in the afternoon, and in the evening is a journalist, a telephone operator, or a teacher. Such men uncomplainingly support huge families of sick, idle, or unsuccessful relations who sit about talking, stand around in bars, stroll up and down alone, gamble, or even lie in bed. To be a little ill is a career in itself. There are the men who get up only at night. There are others who see how many meals they can do without. One of the most amusing Madrileños I ever met told me that he never allowed anything to interfere with his "profession," which was to be an observer of life and an avoider of effort. He was middle-aged and a qualified doctor. He was idle on principle. He lived on very little. His friends fed him. At a period of financial crisis he was nearly persuaded to take on the idlest of jobs with a famous foreign surgeon. He refused it when he discovered, just in time, that he would have to walk up and down three flights of stairs every day when he came to the surgeon's flat. The only single-purpose man missing in Madrid is the student of nature. About plants, trees, birds, and animals the Madrileño is incurious and indifferent: except for the bull, an animal is nothing to him. The lost dog starves and dies on the building lot.

In this Madrid where we have been walking we have noticed certain buildings in rose-coloured brick with low-pitched, red-tiled roofs and wide eaves. To the streets these red buildings bring the flush of pleasure. Among them the Prado, faced by the stone of Colmenar and with

149

great cedars shading its green lawns, is pre-eminent. That corner of Madrid by the Prado is an oasis in a city that is often burning and too brilliant for all the water that is swooshed onto the avenues by the hoses or that trickles in the irrigation channels under the trees. The best things in Madrid convey gravity and a familiar grace. The Prado has not the official oppressiveness of a museum. In Spain the individual, and the family, have always been more important than the State, which is by turns feared, used, exploited, and trampled on like a hotel carpet; and it is natural to Spain that the Prado should be, fundamentally, not a museum, but a private collection of pictures assembled by Hapsburg monarchs who happened to collect at the height of Spanish wealth and power. The Spaniards like to point out that, unlike the other great European galleries, the Prado contains no stolen pictures. Nothing looted in war. To all their pictures they have an indisputable private title. On this point they are almost snobbish.

The Prado is not the best-lit gallery in the world, but it is the least wearying. In it are the best Velázquezes in the world, and it claims to have more Tintorettos and Titians than there are in Italy. There is a superb collection of Flemish pictures. There are Breughels. There are the strange pictures of Hieronymus Bosch which engaged the religious mania of Philip II. The Prado is not well provided with French, Dutch, or German paintings, and there are hardly any English, but in the Spanish school one has the whole spiritual history of Spain in Ribera, Zurbarán, Murillo, El Greco, Velázquez, and Goya. To Goya we look most of all, for Madrid is his city. It is a special experience to go from the Prado to see the Goya frescoes in the church of San Antonio beyond the north station. The church is a little museum now, but at its replica nearby, the girls still come to pray to San Antonio to give them lovers. It is the favourite place for those popular weddings which begin so stiffly and which end in the party walking the streets to shouts of "Long live the bride, long live the mother of the bride, long live the sister of the bride," and so on. They will dance in the cafés out at Cuatro Caminos to the radio and the electric organ.

Madrid stays up later, gets up later, does everything later, than any other capital in Europe. The Madrileño hates the clock, and indeed, except for the sacred clock over the old Ministry of the Interior in the Puerta del Sol, all the clocks in Madrid are wrong. Often hours wrong. "What time is it," a maid calls from the window to another maid down below, "two o'clock or four o'clock?" The zealous Falange party leaders burst out every so often and attempt to change these habits. A new minister gives an order that all civil servants are to be at their offices by nine. He is at once christened "the abominable nine-o'clock man." There is no getting the Madrileño to eat his heavy lunch before two or two-thirty or to go back to his shop or office before five. He dines at ten.

But because the new Madrid is much more a worker's city than it used to be, it shows signs of doing things earlier at night. The real source of changing custom is inflation and the very high cost of living. So the fashionable performance at the theatre or cinema is now the one at seven, and no longer the one at eleven o'clock. A new law forbids

151

theatres to remain open after one-thirty. Inflation is driving people out of restaurants, the popular *tascas* or eatinghouses, into snack bars and cafeterias: the bars increase every year, the cafés decline. More standing, less sitting, lighter meals in the evening.

In the Victorian age and up to thirty years ago the people of Madrid ate enormous meals—that is to say, all people who ate at all; for Spaniards still belong to two races: those who eat and those who don't. In the Cerralbo house, there are the menus of the family—they are unbelievable in the number of courses; but I have many times sat down in humble pensions to a luncheon of huge helpings of hors d'oeuvres, soup, fish, some regional dish, followed by chicken, steak, sweet cake, and fruit. The fat men of Madrid were one of the sights of the nation as they almost lay under their ballooning bellies in the cafés or moved slowly down the Calle de Alcalá with sadness of grounded planets. Lately I have noticed only one survivor of this brotherhood. He was old, drunk, and, to an indifferent café full of people, was denouncing oratorically "this famous modern world." But the smart cocktail parties do not begin till eight and go on till ten or eleven. First Madrid copied "*el* five o'clock tea" (at seven) from Europe; the *apéritif* was almost unknown. Now the Madrileño drinks Italian vermouth, gins of peculiar mark, and whiskey. He is still an abstemious drinker. His real drink is black coffee, at all hours. It has ceased to be good because real coffee is expensive, but in the old cafés it is still served with a glass of water—the delicious mountain water of Madrid, which many of the exiles longed for after the Civil War. Chocolate drinking—the strong cinnamon chocolate served in small cups and as sweet as real Turkish coffee—has almost died out.

The Madrileño is in all things torn between his traditional habits and the new notions of the modern, international world. If there are crowds on the brassy Gran Via, in the pseudo luxury of the new cafés that look like Hollywood sets, there are also numbers of people in the narrow, ill-lit back streets of the older part of the city eating in the *tascas*. some of these have smartened up under the influence of tourism, and are losing their Spanish simplicity. The true *tasca* is often a rough-looking, humble place. You go into a small, dark bar full of shouting men who stand by the zinc counter. The shouting barman slops down small glasses of Valdepeñas wine, five at a time. The eating room of the *tasca* is off the bar, a place with a stone floor, possibly, and always a wall of Talavera tiles. You eat off a marble slab, or perhaps they will bring a tablecloth. No elegance. Room for about a dozen customers. The company is mostly male, the tiles give an echo to the loud voices.

You will eat suckling pig in some *tascas* that specialize in it. You will eat the best fish of the Biscayan coast or the Mediterranean. If Spanish sole has not the quality of Dover sole, the hake is unsurpassed; this fish, so humble in northern countries, is here transformed. There is bream baked in chilies and garlic, there are the mullets, the prawns, the *langostinos*, and oysters. In the good *tascas* one eats famous dishes like *cocido*, that fine clear stew of pork, chicken, leek, potatoes, and chickpeas, the mountainous *paellas* of rice, saffron, peppers, and mussels, or those

153

powerful orange-coloured stews of Asturian sausage. The *tasca* may be a slum bar packed with lorry drivers or market men, like the ones at the bottom of the Calle de Toledo near the fish market, but the food is pure and good. The Madrileño is quarrelsome and critical if his food is not as it should be. He does not argue with the waiter or the proprietor; he calls the cook.

The people who go to the *tascas* are of all classes, the very rich and the modest, the aristocrat, the banker, the professor, the petit bourgeois; once at table they are *en famille*, barking at each other. It is in the genius of the Madrileño that he puts his personality before his caste. Below the *tascas* are the old seventeenth-century *posadas* or muleteer's taverns in the neighbourhood of Cava Baja, where the market people and peasants come and stay in the galleried courtyards where the washing drips. The shops in this neighbourhood sell harness and tobacco sieves; Madrid is a city of small shops. These *posadas* are outposts of Castile, and Castile is poor; the rank, sour life of the villages seeps in—those crumbling villages which now the peasants are leaving.

We are a long way from the Ritz, from Horcher's and El Jockey, a long way from the smart patisseries, from Lhardy's, where one meets that Edwardian grace which Madrid has preserved longer than any other city. For how much longer? At Lhardy's lately I listened to right-wing personages talking about the decay of the regime. They know the Spanish future is precariously in the hands of the world outside.

There were Edwardian vestiges in cafés like Varela,

one of the last of the famous ones to go, at the end of Preciados (the Madrileño does not habitually use the word for "street"); Pombo's went soon after the war. The bars have suffered less; the old ones in Echegaray and other streets nearby, where the flamenco singers, the dancers, the bullfighters go, are dead by day but roaring by night. The floor is deep in prawn shells and sugar papers; the wineglasses ring; the male voices bellow and rebound from the gaudy, tiled walls where perhaps a bull's head looks down, or some crude fresco of the life and death of Manolete, the almost sainted bullfighter. Men are meeting in that traditional chest-to-chest, backslapping hug of the Spanish male, shouting in each other's faces. In the back room the hired guitarists are strumming to the flamenco songs. But the bull's head on the wall may mislead the traveller who wishes everything Spanish to be "typical"; behind the bar, among the bottles, are the results of the football lottery. The great football players are as well known as the bullfighters, and in the economic revolution through which Madrid is passing, football is a cheap spectacle, and the bull ring is exorbitantly expensive. Bars, the cinema, football, are the new distractions of Madrid. The brothels have been closed. The peculiarity of the brothels was an absurd quality of homeliness; half the men who went to them did so to talk business and politics and to gossip, to wait for something *muy español* to happen.

Yet the "typical" distractions have survived the puritan discouragement of them in the years immediately after the Civil War. The guitars talk across the stage of a night club and gradually silence the room as the climax becomes clearer, quicker, peremptory. The singers and dancers sit around as if they were waiting for some parlour game to begin. That little Arab child from Granada will soon get up, and as she stands, the childish smile goes from her face, she lowers the lids of her smoky eyes, fixes a scowl between her brows, and then, with high-tempered fingers snapping, stamps fiercely into the dance. These girls turn into savages; they arch their thin backs like bending bows, their heads shake in temper, and their heels talk fast in a mutter of hostility. These flamenco and Gypsy dances elicit all the incitement and defiance in sexual passion. They are the direct language of the body, unperverted by lewdness of the mind.

Whatever the performance, whether the curious strangled notes of the *cante jondo* are being torn from a falsetto voice or whether the crisis of the dance is achieved and dissipated, there are grace and insolence in the women, cruelty and mastery, absolute male conceit and dominance, in the men. "*Lele, lele, lele—*" the singer begins, and strikes that sigh of hollow sadness, the hard sigh of the fatal transience of pleasure, love, and delight. Even in the conquering, sardonic songs in which cunning makes a fool of love, where jealousy revels in its own evil, vengeance in its own emptiness, or pleasure in its brevity and deceits, the falling minor chords of the Spanish musical genre are there in all their melancholy insinuation.

A sign of the present restlessness in Madrid, caused by the granting of a little more freedom, is the cautious revival of the theatre. After the Civil War (*nuestra guerra:* our war, they call it, being fatally obliged to have a war the

Spanish way and not the way of the rest of the world),
the theatre died in Madrid. Many theatres closed perma-
nently. Now, by collecting a small tax on the royalties of
authors, two of the finest theatres in Madrid have been
handsomely refurbished, and the first night of a popular
zarzuela—a musical play—is a glittering occasion. There
are now two State-subsidized theatres, one for the classical
drama—though here foreign dramatists like Arthur Miller
and T. S. Eliot have so far preponderated over the Spanish
classics—and another for Spanish contemporaries. There are
a number of respectable new dramatists, and there is a
distinct effervescence in the experimental theatre—despite
the ecclesiastical censorship, which applies to literature as
well and is far more severe than the political censorship.
I have heard a young Spanish dramatist take a perverse
pride in the censor, as if he could not write without an
enemy. All the same, Madrid is not the city to which any
traveller goes for its contemporary arts. They can flourish
only timidly in the artificial conditions under which ideas
have to be conceived. The interesting thing is that there is
enough restiveness to make the theatre stir.

And restive the new Madrid is. It has become self-
conscious. The apathy which followed the Civil War has
gone. A younger generation has grown up which did not
know that war and is bored by talk of it. There is less fear
in political conversation. The spies of the police state have
become pathetic. "And No. 59?" you hear the spy ask
the lift boys at the hotels. They palm him off with the
formula: "*Muy discreto*"—and shrug their shoulders with
contempt. Large numbers of the increasing body of uni-

versity students, housed in the fine new university residences, go abroad. They come back demanding what the students of others countries have: ordinary freedom. There are no politics in Spain at the moment; there is a vacuum; but as one Spaniard has said, they are beginning to feel "the biological need for freedom." They are eager, sharp-minded, and bored. Madrid is a city which would perhaps still prefer to be in the nineteenth century; but now it is modern in aspect, it wants to be modern in mind as well. It is beginning to feel that tension which is the essence of city life.

Yet it would be a mistake to think that the traditional Madrid is dead. It has never been a museum. Famous old streets like the Calle de Toledo, running out of the city, are full of thriving life. The Rastro or flea market is packed tight and black with thousands of people on Sundays, buying everything from wardrobes and cheap furniture to old shoes, new clothes, and antiques. The markets roar. Life pullulates in the warren-like slums. The blind tap along; a woman strides beside a pair of dwarfs; a laughing deaf-and-dumb couple hold up the crowd; workmen charge into the bars and order their morning brandy; the radio shouts out the latest flamenco song. At night these iron-grey streets are sour and dark and severe; they are dangerous to walk in because, lately, enterprising people have been ripping up the hydrants and selling them!

It is in these ill-lit streets of thousands of small shops or staring, shabby doorways that the Madrileños like to wander. They know their city. They regard it with that homely affection all Spaniards feel for their own towns.

They feel about it domestically, as they feel for their family and their friends. They never boast about it. They neglect it with love. They have nothing like the civic pride of a Parisian, a Londoner, or a New Yorker. Madrid is a familiar place, entirely personal, without loneliness. It must be the only city without loneliness in the world.

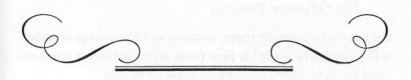

SEVILLE

Take a blind man out of Castile in the spring, put him on the Tierra de María Santissima, the plain of short green corn and rye grass outside Seville, and he will know at once he is in Andalusia and on the way to that city. He will know by the smell of the air. The harsh and stinging odours of lavender and thyme have gone. Now he is walking or driving no longer, but is being lifted or wafted towards the city on air that has ceased to be air and has become a languid melting of the oils and essences of orange blossom and the rose, of jasmin and the myrtle. And although in the city itself he will meet again the strong native reeks of Spanish life—something compounded of olive oil, charcoal, cigar smoke, urine, horse dung, incense, and coffee—the flowers of Andalusia will powerfully and

161

voluptuously overrule them, the rose and the orange blossom will blow hotly upon his face from walls and street corners, until he reels with a nose-knowledge of Seville.

It is even more dizzying to the eyes. As we come across the hedgeless flat country, we see a low-built, Oriental city of roof gardens rising innocently like a tray of white china, chipped here and there by tender ochres. We see the tops of the palms sprouting like pashas in the squares. Inside the city white walls are buried in bougainvillea and wisteria and all climbing flowers, geraniums hanging from thousands of white balconies, great lilies in windows, carnations at street corners, and roses climbing up the walls and even the trees, so that all the gasps and hyperbole of pleasure are on our lips. In a minute we are voluptuaries. In two minutes our walk slackens into a dawdle. In three minutes we are looking for a foot of shade. And gazing at the oranges on the trees by the trolley-bus stop, we ask ourselves how it is that in a city like this people do not pick them as they go by, how trains can be got out of the lazy station, lorries unload at the port on the Guadalquivir where ships have come up seventy miles from the sea, or how any of the inhabitants do anything but sigh, sit down, or sleep.

Andalusia is the home of Spanish lyrical poetry. Delight, magic, enchantment, all the words suggested by little fountains playing in cool courtyards, come monotonously to the poets. George Borrow, who saw the Inquisition at every corner of this city, confessed that as he stood by the rose walls of the Alcázar he burst into tears of rapture. His rage had gone. But we need other words than delight, rapture, and enchantment to define the city. What is there in the spirit of the Sevillano that breaks the burden of so much sensual beauty and saves him from Oriental torpor? Certainly he sleeps in the afternoon and talks half the night, but he is notoriously the liveliest, most sparkling of creatures, the cleverest monkey, his enemies would say, in Spain. Ask the enemies of Seville to define it. They reply at once with tolerant contempt: "A city of actors." Seville is theatre. It is totally a stage. Lope de Vega, the greatest of the Spanish dramatists, called it "the proud theatre of the world," and in its richest days, when Columbus came back from his first voyage to America and before its 16,000 silk looms had been silenced by the wool trade of Castile and the glut of Pizarro's gold, there was nothing bombastic in the phrase.

The legendary figures by whom we know Seville are all theatrical: it is the city of Don Juan, of Figaro, and of Carmen—but we must say this last discreetly because it annoys the Sevillanos: they have had enough of Carmen. Cervantes, not a native of the city, was in trouble there—as elsewhere—and caught enough of the spirit of the place to get himself thrown out of the cathedral for protesting against a statue. A place, he saw, for gestures, like Don Juan's. The painters who were born or lived there—Velázquez and Zurbarán—were respectable; and Murillo, the true painter of the women of the city, caught the softer aspect of it: the flowered, moonlit sweetness. But the legendary pagans like Peter the Cruel and Don Miguel de Mañara came straight from the stage. The monstrosities committed by Peter the Cruel are as sordid as any in history; the interesting thing is what the dramatic instinct of the Sevillano did with them. One of his notorious murders occurred at night in a silent street of the labyrinth called Santa Cruz. There was only one witness—an old woman who went to her window, candle in hand, and saw his face for a second. The street is still called the street of the candlestick—Candillejo. But Mañara comes even closer to our notions of the emotional extremity to which the Sevillian character can run and illustrates how it tends to give men a single purpose which utterly absorbs them for a time, and may, at a shock, turn with equal singleness in the opposite direction.

Don Miguel de Mañara was once thought to be the original of Don Juan. The idea was mistaken. He was not born when the original play portraying the character was written. Mañara was a rake who repented, but in truly Sevillian fashion; he was not content with an ordinary act of remorse. He had to make the fine gesture and enact the awful scene. From wealth, lust, and riot he turned suddenly to the contemplation of death. Pursuing a veiled woman in the street at night, he pulled the veil off her face and a death's head stared at him. He encountered a funeral in the street and, lifting the cloth of the bier, saw that the corpse was himself. When he came to repentance, it was in the great manner. He built a splendid Charity Hospital for the Poor which still exists, and there at the entrance one can see the stone of a Sevillano who was an actor forever. The inscription reads: "Here lies the body of the worst man who ever lived." The worst! Nothing less would satisfy him as a curtain line.

It would be fanciful to see Seville only through its past

fantasies, its amorous brawlers, its thousands of witty barbers, its dangerous cigarette girls, and its penitents. Seville was once a Roman capital and, after the discovery of America, it also produced that reserved and grave masculine character, the empire builder; so that often in Seville one sees examples of those reserved, dignified, grave Roman types, excellent in the saddle, family-proud, and conscious of occasion, who look like southern forerunners of the imperial kind of Englishman turned out by Dr. Arnold. Even the clubs of Seville recall those of Pall Mall, except that the windows are wide open, so that the members are in the front row of the stalls. No one ever reads a book in these clubs; twice as many members are fast asleep as in any club in London, and the waistline is more abandoned. Trousers have to be cut high and wide to accommodate the great globe below. A belt would slip down and expose all that owning bull farms and olive groves can do to the figure. But even these men, stunned by the blessings and martyrdoms of obesity, will get to their feet about midday and proceed like slowed-down planets to the barbers to be clipped, shaved, and oiled, to hear what rascalities Figaro has to tell them; or will stand in Sierpes, where no traffic ever runs, and argue dramatically with their friends. Roman Seville is full of the old Andalusian Adam. A street scene in the perpetual play is what they love to enact or watch. The last time I was in Sierpes I saw a small procession of youths and children and a couple of policemen moving towards me. Its centre was a young drunken American who, happily, spoke some Spanish, for he was able to put on quite a show for the crowd, who were teasing him. A little girl of ten was having a battle of wits with him. He stood up to them all so well that they accompanied him like an admiring and mischievous court. Only the policemen gave up. Reluctantly they had to keep a point with their sergeant elsewhere. All occurrences are revered, the small and the very great.

So it is fitting that at Corpus Christi the choir boys should dance their medieval dance before the high altar of the Cathedral; it is fitting that when this cathedral was built to celebrate the triumph of Spain in freeing Western Europe from Islam, it was made the largest Gothic cathedral in the world. And today it is natural that the processions of Holy Week should be the most extraordinary religious spectacles to be seen in Europe since the fourteenth century. Thousands of foreigners come to see it, but they are swallowed up by the whole population of the city, nearly 400,000 people, who are out in the streets for a week, living and acting the whole display. Spectacle is in the blood. What the state occasion is to the British, what the historical pageant is to the Germans, and the parade to the Americans, the religious pageant is to the Spaniards, and to the Sevillano most of all.

The first distinctive quality of Holy Week in Seville lies in the Sevillano and Sevillana themselves. They do not think of themselves as simply natives of the place or as a number of separate creatures who happen to live and work there. Each one feels himself to be the whole city. All Spaniards feel this about their native place, but the Sevillano carries it to a point at once exquisite and absurd. His feeling is rhetorical, yet, even more, his sense of the city is

intimate and domestic. All Seville is his house. The streets
are the living quarters, the squares are where he meets his
friends, the little Baroque churches are his gilded drawing
rooms. It is extraordinary, if one happens to visit or stay in
one, how silent and empty-seeming the houses are. A face
at a window, a servant going upstairs, a figure alone in
rooms darkened to keep out the sun—there is not much
more sense of habitation than that. People eat there and
sleep there, they water flowers on the balcony—but not
there, one supposes, do they live. And so, when the processions of Holy Week begin, the Sevillano is no spectator; he
is of them. They are part of his personal drama.

Even if we go only by the number, length, duration, and
membership of the processions, we see how completely
they pervade. Are all Sevillanos passionately religious? No.
Has the Church enemies after the Civil War? Yes, very
many. Do some people deplore the processions, pointing
to the enormous amount of convent, church, and religious
monument building of the last twenty years in a poor
country that lacks the will or the talent to do more than
nibble lazily at its worst social problems? Many do so deplore. Yet because the processions are theatre, eyes brighten
and the arguments vanish. In each parish church there is a
cofradía, or brotherhood—they are exclusively male institutions—which maintains the elaborate and beautifully
carved and golden floats on which the image of the Virgin
patroness or the Christ is carried. Some *cofradías* maintain
two or even three of these floats. They are objects of pride,
for some of the figures are by the great Spanish sculptors—
Montañes, Hito del Castillo, the Roldáns, Alonso Cano,

are among them—who excelled in the dramatic realism of their work. One or two are masterpieces, and, listening to the crowd, one sees that whether they respond to the religious meaning or not, they respond to the craftsmanship and to the expressiveness of the figures in the scenes of the Crucifixion. There are something like fifty of these *cofradías* in Seville. Their membership is large. It is not always easy to become a member. Parents are known to put their sons' names down for them at birth. Some of the *cofradías* originated in the guilds of the Middle Ages, and their popular trade names have stuck to them: cigarette makers, bakers, roadmakers, and so on. Beginning on the Monday before Easter, the *cofradías* in turn bear the floats through the streets from their parish and then along a set route in the centre to the Cathedral; the procession pauses there, and then the return journey begins. Some of the processions are eight or eleven hours on their route and go on through the night—first a posse of the municipal guard, then barefoot penitents carrying their lighted torches, the standard S.P.Q.R., banners, acolytes swinging the smoking censers, and then the image at last, followed by a band. For half a mile the members of the *cofradía* precede the image in their conical hats with eye slits and in robes, carrying their candles. After a week of this the streets are glazed with candle grease. The making of the show is its slowness, for each float is borne on the shoulders of thirty-six men concealed beneath the velvet curtains below, who shuffle forward in the heat from fifty to a hundred yards at a spell. They work like galley slaves. The very slowness of the progress means that they effectually occupy the main part of the city and entirely close its

168

centre. The crowds hang about and then suddenly someone shouts: "Here comes San Vincente" or "Here comes Santa Cruz," and the neighbourhood of the Cathedral is packed and impenetrable. On Good Friday the climax is reached. Famous images like the Macarena, which excites an extraordinary fervour in the crowd, or the Jesús del Gran Poder, which draws out its admiration, pass into the Cathedral. The *Miserere* of the composer Eslava is sung in a last orgy of theatrical magnificence and, to crown all, a peal of artificial thunder booms and rebounds in the enormous edifice.

There is nothing more to be said of the stage management of Holy Week; it is the play that counts, its peculiar quality of penetrating into the daily life of the people. The Sevillano, like all other Spaniards, is addicted to repetition and the monotonous; he wakes up only at the high moments. There, as in the dance, in the bullfights, in his songs, he is taut and silent and most critical. He is the man of the crisis. In singing or the dance, the guitar mutters away monotonously, playing on the nerves, slackening off in order, with dramatic suddenness, to deceive and to enhance, until the torpor of the audience is broken down and the singer or dancer can electrify him by wit or take him by storm. Something like that takes place in the processions. The high moments occur when the image leaves its church, when it enters the Cathedral, when it leaves, and, finally, when in an uproar of enthusiasm it returns to the family possession of its parish. That moment of the return, if it should happen (as it often does) to be at two or three in the morning, is superb.

You have been hanging about in some bar drinking beer

in the heat of the night, and presently in the crowd outside
there is pushing and scrambling and flurry: the sound of
drum taps is coming nearer. The streets are narrow—in
some of them there is only room for a carriage; many are
only alleys—the houses are chalk white, the starlit sky is
black. The breath of the flowers is cool and oily. The
street lights are put out and the walls are lit only by the
candles of the hundreds of penitents in their hoods and
robes and by the scores of candles on the image. The
windows are crowded. People stand along the roof gardens.
The simple façade of the church, with its Baroque scroll,
looks like a strong gracious face, for though they may be
like drawing rooms inside, the churches of Seville have those
well-found and noble walls which Spaniards still have the
custom and art of building. The candles round the Virgin
flutter, and her affecting doll's face shines out of her
headdress and her jewelled velvet robes. She stands, certainly like a queen, under her canopy. Eyes sparkle in the
crowd. The prettiness, the peep-show prettiness, delights
the Sevillano. He has an almost childish excitement before
pretty things. And now, before the image is carried in, there
is sudden silence. The small voice of a singer rises. He is
singing a *saeta*, one of those weird traditional "deep songs"
which seem to be the music of a man in complete solitude,
a personal cry of strangled passion and loneliness, and
whose words are a naïve mingling of self and religion, Arab
lyricism and the love of the city. The falsetto voice,
whinnying and gulping its minutely broken syllables, is half
Arab, but also half Gypsy, for the final vowel *a* is drawn
out into that curious grunting *aun* of the Gypsy singing.

The pauses in the song are there so that we shall be astonished by a sudden cruel heightening of crisis which breaks
at last into the downhill rush of fulfilment. The words are
not hard to catch. They are essentially declarations of love:
the singer is singing his personal praise of the Virgin, saying that she is the prettiest of all and the pride of the
proudest and most beautiful city on earth. It is said that in
recent years the *saetas* have become more extravagant and
have travelled a long way from traditional simplicity. The
tendency in all Spain in the last twenty years is to "pile it
on" in a manner one can't but think decadent. (I notice
that old bullfight fans complain that whereas the crowd in
Seville was once unique in Spain, in freezing into con-
temptuous silence when the *torero* made some ghastly mistake or lost his nerve, now it has lost the classical dignity
and shouts with the worst.) Even so, if the modern
Spanish tendency is to overdo things and run into vulgarity,
there is no doubt that dramatic extravagance is in the
Sevillian nature.

But the high moments of the processions that pervade
the city in this week are few. The night scene before the
Cathedral is magnificent. Floodlighting turns this tremendous domed, buttressed, and towered building, where the
stained glass blazes at night, into something fabulous. The
smoking incense and the candlelight transform the crowd.
All this is high drama. But when one looks at the whole
thing, hour by hour, one notices that the normal character
of the processions is slack, dawdling, and familiar. An
American will be shocked by the slowness, a German by
the lack of precision, an Englishman by the absence of

dignity. There is nothing of the rehearsed occasion. The penitents lounge, their candles and hoods at all angles, the bands play popular waltzing marches—I noticed again and again that they play a slow military version of "The Maiden's Prayer"—the crowd pushes through the ranks. Even in the Cathedral, where an inured Protestant like myself expects a certain *tenue,* I have seen one or two penitents get and answer messages from the congregation— "See you at So-and-So later on"—and in bars I have seen a thirsty young penitent pull off his hood, gulp down a beer, and rush back to his place. Occasionally young boys appear in the processions, and one will see an anxious mother and a father on his dignity go up to their son and put his hood straight. And when the image is set down for a rest, the sweating bearers beneath naturally lift the curtains and squat on the ground getting a breath of air. The water sellers crowd round them with jars, people give them cigarettes, and wives or sisters will rush up to give them sandwiches or a cup of coffee. In the meantime the bearers are grinning and cursing and making wisecracks at the crowd, for the Sevillano does not miss an opportunity in this game. This easy familiarity is not only delightful; it is of the very essence of the *popular* spirit which the Spanish have preserved to an extent I have seen nowhere else in the world. The proudest of all people, they are the most at ease with each other and quite classless—in the ordinary relations of life the most classless people I know.

And this ease of theirs in the great occasion comes out in another way. They know at what points a procession will be prettiest or most dramatic. They know that the

procession of Santa Cruz is exquisite after it has turned off
the boulevard just above Carmen's tobacco factory, now
the university, and passes under the rich trees of the gardens
beyond the rose walls of the Alcázar, its candlelight
glittering and its incense smoking under the acacias, its
music diffused in the gardens. Others know that at points
in Sierpes or some other narrow street barely wide enough
for the float, it will be set momentarily like a shrine; or
that in the square called San Salvador it will stand against
the huge dwarfing walls of great churches. They know
where the most curious of all, the Silent Procession, is best
seen. This familiar knowledge of what is felicitous, where
the charming moments are, is a sign of how they own their
city street by street, knowing the character of each part of
it. Once more, we see the Sevillanos' talent and taste for the
small pleasures of life, and for thinking the local thing is
the one to be cherished most. Smallness is important to
them. One can tell that by their speech—whenever they
can, they use a diminutive: not a glass of wine, but a
little glass; not a snack of fried squid, shrimp sausage, or
tiny silver eels from the North, with their glass of man-
zanilla, but a *little* snack; and if they want more than that,
a dish of it, then the dish becomes a *little* dish, flowers become *little* flowers, birds singing in their cages on the walls
of the patio become *little* birds; even bulls become *little*
bulls. Smaller and smaller things become in their minds,
until they have reached the imaginary tininess of childish
delight.

Yet, as I said earlier, the people of Seville are not awed
spectators of their show; they are part of it. If you go into

any of the churches when a particular procession is over, on any of the days following, you will find scores of people coming to admire the floats and particularly those famous as works of art. These churches all have something of the family house about them; there is always something going on, and anyone, any passing stranger, will eagerly show you its curiosities. One morning in the Triana —the Gypsy quarter on the other bank of the Guadalquivir —in the Santa Anna, the oldest church in the city, they had put a ladder over the altar and were changing the Virgin's clothes, tying on her many bodices and petticoats and getting her ready for an ordination service in the afternoon. This church looks like a picture shop. Its choir and organ carvings are good, but it also has the usual haphazard collection of antique oddities. One of the strangest was an image of the Virgin presented in the nineteenth century by the Duc de Montpensier, the patron and friend of Alexandre Dumas. The Spaniards do not care much for French importations, and this one embarrasses them. The Virgin is portrayed in the fashionable clothes of a society woman at a reception or the races. The verger looked dubiously at it, but, a true Sevillano, he had an eye for the bizarre. By the altar stood a fine grandfather's clock. Rich Spaniards had a craze for collecting fine English clocks at the end of the eighteenth century, and their families have dumped these curiosities in the nearest church. One finds them everywhere. Once more one sees that the churches are one more room in the family life of the city.

On Thursday of Holy Week, the shops close and now the whole of the city is out and crowds swarm in on the

country buses. At five in the afternoon the popular *paseo*
begins, the ritual of walking up and down. Until now the
women had been present but inconspicuous. The Sevillana
is small and plump and pale, inclined to roundness and
heaviness in the face and, until she talks, without light in
her eyes. Beside the male, whether of the grave Roman
type or the jumping cracker, the lady is placid and demure.
But on Thursday the sex suddenly grows a foot taller.
They have taken off their flat slippers and shoes—so convenient for the cobbles of this cobbled place—and have put
on their high heels, their high combs, and their black
mantillas. One blinks. Women who were unnoticeable the
day before have suddenly become beauties, coolly conscious of a part to play. A hidden pride has come out. They
rarely, one notices, deign to talk to their escorts. After
Holy Week is out, in the excitement of the Feria, they will
change again. They will be clapping hands, snapping
thumbs and fingers, clacking the castanets in the night-
long dances that go on in the *casetas*, the family marquees
and avenues by the Park. It will be a new play of whirling
and stamping pleasure.

The civilization that Seville has inherited is a good deal
Arab. Almost all the older things in Seville were built by
Arab craftsmen and, although modern blocks of flats have
gone up, the main domestic part of the city is based on the
Arab patio or courtyard. There is a strong white wall, and
the rooms open onto a central court. The streets of Santa
Cruz wind and tangle. They are built to catch only glanc-
ing blows of the terrible Spanish sun, to be channels of
cool air, and the names of these streets are set out in the

175

large black classical letters of centuries ago, and are dramatic in their direct and simple evocations. Streets are called, quite plainly: Air, Water, Bread, Straw, the Dead Moor, Glory, Barabbas, Mosque, Jewry, and Pepper. No fantastications in that heroic age. The Spaniards of the Reconquest were simple men. In the Gypsy quarter of the Triana, the traditional home of bullfighters, dancers, and singers, the main street is called Pureza—Purity. It is one of the clues to the character of the Sevillano that even in modern streets he has not changed his lettering. It is superior to that of any city in the world, and it emphasizes how important place and locality are to the Sevillian temperament. No search for identity here: the Sevillano is a man and, as Don Juan said when he posted his name on a wall, if anyone wants anything of him, here he is. The streets of Seville are clean; even the poor streets are clean. There is no filth in the Triana. One breathes flower-borne air as one passes the grilled windows and gates of the houses and looks into the courtyards. From the modest patios to those of the greater houses, the cool ferns stand there on the tiles and the flowers are massed. These patios are really open rooms, often with chairs and tables in them, and under the gallery in the house of some well-off lawyer or family who do well out of the olive oil or the sherry trade, one sees the best pictures of the house and the finest furniture standing virtually in the open. Silent always, mysterious, and as if entranced by their own flowers, the patios are little stage sets, little peep shows in themselves. They display the pride of the family as well as its natural pleasure in living in the open air.

In the Feria, those who can afford it hire or build *casetas*, wooden booths or marquees, near the Park. The *caseta* has a "living room" in the front and a kitchen concealed behind it; the living room is separated from the street by a low rail, and there many families move elegant pieces of furniture from their houses—armoires, sideboards, handsome dining tables. Pictures hang on the wall. Publicly, with some air of consequence, the family lives in the open for the Feria and takes enormous family pride in keeping open house, inviting the passing strangers as well as their friends to drink with them. There is no rough-and-ready camping about this. They are here to be seen at their best and in abandoned gaiety, drinking and dancing all through the night. In the Feria there is the procession of carriages to watch. Remarkable and luxurious equipages go by drawn by their teams of fine horses. The great families own them; the less-great hire them. At this time one sees the parade of riders formally dressed in the Andalusian style—the low-crowned Córdoba hat, the short jacket that sets off the waist of the rider, the tight trousers with the florid leather facings, and, behind the riders, the girls in their long red-and-white dresses, their combs, and the roses or carnations in the hair.

So well known is this that when the foreigner thinks of Spain, he thinks of this Sevillian scene, hears the castanets and the tambourines and the speed of the tossing music of the Sevillana. Spain is, of course, quite unlike this. This is a purely Sevillian scene, and it has spread abroad that legend of romantic Spain which has infuriated so many Spanish writers. There is, one has to say, something very provincial in this city. Its habits and manners are set. The stranger must not get the impression that the gaiety he sees will pass the bounds of formality, even when it appears at its wildest. The very wildness has its rules. Spanish life is profoundly unromantic. Overwhelmingly it is ruled—as the theatre is ruled—by the strict sense of genre and local style. Things change, of course. Seville has become an important river port. The Vespas roar in the streets; the old grinding yellow trams have gone and have been replaced by the trolley bus. Young girls go in for blond hair dips. And lovers, sitting among the roses in the park, are bolder. It is now permissible for them to hold hands or put an arm round a waist. Many of those lovely houses in Santa Cruz are let out in flats. The bullfights are rarely good, for this spectacle has its terrible periods of boredom, when the bulls are bad or the *torero* incompetent. There are plenty of people in the crowd coming away from the bull ring complaining of the enormous prices charged, the commercialization of the show, and the decline of its quality. Foreigners who not often used to go now swarm in, and there is a good deal more of showiness than the rigour of the game. Foreign writers who have become fans of the bullfight have a lot to answer for.

But, in defence of the provinciality of Seville and its contented incuriosity toward the outside world, this must be said: Provinciality has preserved the Sevillano and enhances his local genius. He is incurably an actor and a mocker. "Come on, Gypsy," calls out one Gypsy, derisively, to another in the street. He loves to shout a compliment to a woman, and prides himself on the neatness of it. To a very tall woman, a workman shouted: "Come by tomorrow so that we can see the other half." The *piropo*, or public compliment, is now supposedly illegal—it annoyed foreigners—but it has not entirely vanished. Wit, the invention of conceits, are irrepressible in the Sevillano; he loves riposte and fantasy. At the height of Holy Week, when the crowds were thickest and the café tables almost filled one little square, I heard two rival shrimp-and-crab sellers shouting at each other from their stalls on opposite sides of the square. One was making up fantastic eulogies, full of astute local references, of his shrimps that came from Cádiz; his opponent listened carefully; the crowd was almost silent and then burst into admiring laughter. Then it was the turn of the other, a man from Alicante, who let fly with his own fantasy. The crowd was entranced. The act went on for half an hour, a real battle of comical words between two cities. I wish I had written it down, but it was going too fast for me and both parties were helpless with laughter. Make a light passing remark to any inhabitant of this place and he will outstrip you in a flash. "How are you this morning?" you say to the cab driver, expecting a mild little "Very well, thank you" or a conventional "Fine." That's too dull for the cabman. Skinny himself, he stands up and looks down at his skinny horse, which is soon for the bull ring. "Stupendous!" he says.

Seville is theatre. Great theatre, yet with thousands of little turns and scenes going on on its stage. Its vanity is to be the city of Don Juan; it is in fact far more the city of Figaro, mocking, playing practical jokes, and then dropping off into a self-absorbed yet blank-minded doze until the next wicked or childish opportunity occurs. A place of dignity—and yet I have seen an old gentleman of the gravest kind pick up a sugar castor and, leaning out of the café window where he was sitting, sprinkle another old gentleman's hair with it. I suppose people use the telephone there out of simple respect for the instrument; for their real business they send a boy out with a note to the favourite bar or café of the person it is addressed to. It is a paradise of hangers-on, of doorstep characters who know everything, of people who stop to talk; but do not suppose it is happy-go-lucky and unbusinesslike. The slowest action in the blissfully slow life of Andalusia is the action of letting money pass out of one's hand. Seville put up a considerable struggle to keep the South American gold.

The regions of Spain and their cities have an extreme independence of temperament and, even in the levelling of modern civilization, some of this survives in the attacks of ridicule they jealously make upon one another. When one uses the word "theatre" of Seville, the citizens of other cities read it in the pedantic sense of shallowness, showiness, rhetoric, and the arts of the mountebank. It must be admitted that modern Seville, beyond the Park, is either pretentious or ugly. It reached the depths of decadence at the time of the Exhibition in the 1930's. Seville has no need of rhetoric about its past. In that enormous historical show the city put on in the fifteenth and sixteenth centuries, there were no rhetoricians; it was the time of men of action. All the cities of Europe have great historical claims on our imagination, until we are choked with history. The claim of Seville is truly colossal and world-changing. I do not know whether many people visit the Archives of the Indies, but in that not very interesting building near the Cathedral, one has the shock of knowing what it must have been like to be discoverers and colonists of America. It meant, above all, the work of men of action; explorers, sailors, soldiers, governors, architects, builders, judges. Here, in thousands of white boxes, are their documents: their plans for cities like Buenos Aires, for the forts at Cartagena, for the avenues of Montevideo and the government houses of Peru; the drawings, the leases, the lawsuits, the certificates of governorship, the trials, the executions. Here we can read the reports of Hernán Cortés, the letters of Columbus. And of a failure, too: the long letter of Cervantes, the imprisoned tax collector, failed author, unwanted soldier, and cathedral brawler—applying vainly for a job overseas. Seville played out the great roles; and now that history has passed beyond it, it amuses itself with the little ones, the magic that passes the tedious hours of life.

TURKEY

It was midday. All the torpid and sweetish morning one had been distracted by the shouts of raucous males in the steep street below one's window. Men were selling cakes and bread rolls from the trays or cases on their heads, or goat's milk from the cans carried by their mules. And then, suddenly, sharp at twelve, a louder and prolonged bawling struck up from somewhere in the sky. It was like the noise of a brawl. It came from a minaret close to the hotel. Upon its little balcony stood the muezzin, a shabby young man in jacket and collarless shirt, looking like a factory hand. His hands were cupped to his mouth and he was yelling out: "Great is Allah. Allah alone is God." One was in Istanbul.

Coming from Western Europe, seeing the Bosporus and

hearing that cry for the first time, the traveller exclaims: "The Orient at last!" Coming from Persia or India or Arabia, he says: "Very soon, the West!" Istanbul stands at one of the dramatic junctions of the world. Here two continents come down to the beautiful blue straits and landlocked seas and grind against each other; here two religions and two races jar; and here a huge, dusty, mud-brown city of backbreaking hills, with a skyline of moony domes and minarets, squats across the dividing waters, split into three by the Bosporus, the Golden Horn, and the Sea of Marmara.

Looking south from the ugly European quarter to the Golden Horn, you watch the ferryboats come out and make across the Bosporus. Their smoke trails crisscross on the sheets of water all day long. By night the ferries crawl across like lit-up insects. In a few minutes they will be in Asia. To the east, where the Bosporus narrows on its way to the Black Sea, a strong schoolboy can swim from one continent to another. It is unbelievable. The Turks who boast of it do so incredulously, too—glumly, with fatalism. There is a Bosporus splitting their minds. The educated are Westerners; the mass of people on the Anatolian tableland are living the primitive Asiatic life that has changed little for thousands of years.

Istanbul is no longer the most splendid city in the world. It is no longer Byzantium, the first capital of Christendom. It is no longer Constantinople, chief city of the great Ottoman Empire that once cut deeply into the side of Europe and south into Africa as far as the Sudan. But in situation the city is sublime; it is intrinsically dramatic and hag-ridden, stupefied by its own drama.

When we drink our tea from the samovar and eat our nougat or papery wafers in the neat, fashionable cafés in the narrows of the Bosporus, when we try out our first hubble-bubble pipe there, watching the thousands of bass, mackerel, and mullet being brought off the boats rocking at the quays, we are uneasy. We know we are at the limit of Europe. The forests rising to the Balkans are at our backs; the Soviet Union is around the corner by the Black Sea; before us is the tableland that leads onto the steppe and desert of Asia Minor and of Asia itself.

We are at a key point. No Great Power is going to let another Great Power control these waters. And the key point is ancient. Beyond the Sea of Marmara is the Dardanelles. The Trojan War was fought for this strait, and so was the Gallipoli campaign in the First World War; the twelfth century B.C. and the twentieth A.D. unite in that. All Europe had hated the Turks from the time of the Crusades and from the Turkish capture, in 1453, of the capital of Eastern Christendom, when the great cathedral of Sancta Sophia, far older than St. Peter's, became a mosque; but in the nineteenth and twentieth centuries, when Turkey was "the sick man of Europe" and its empire had almost gone, no one wanted the Turk to be driven off his final strip of European soil. It was safer to let him keep the door key of the gate between Slav, European, Asiatic, and Arab.

And so there is the small sliver of European Turkey, the Turkey of seas and straits—and the Asiatic Turkey of Anatolia, a high bare tableland buttressed by mountains and stretching eastward for, say, a thousand miles to Mount Ararat and the frontiers of Iran. The northern sea-

185

coast is the Black Sea, once colonized by Greeks, a warm, wooded region running past Trebizond to the moist tea plantations on the frontier of Russia. To the south of Ararat lies Iraq; to the southwest is Syria; the southern coast hangs over the eastern end of the Mediterranean and bends around northward to the Greek Aegean.

And the Turk stands there, a prosaic, sober, stubborn, dogged, soldierly man, not quick to speak like the Greeks, not quick to smile, more solid than the excitable Arab races, fatalistic, a distinctly puritanical descendant of the nomadic tribes of Central Asia. (He does not like the word "tribe.") He has been settled on the European straits and the tableland of Anatolia for six hundred years at least. He has been formed, as he settled, by many earlier cultures: Hittite, Phrygian, Persian, Greek, Alexandrian, Roman, and Byzantine; his Hittite carvings, his Greek theatres and cities, his Roman hippodromes, his Byzantine churches, his Crusaders' castles, have made him a custodian of remnants.

Istanbul has meant so much to the imagination that the reality shocks most travellers. We cannot get the sultans out of our minds. We half expect to find them still cross-legged and jewelled on their divans. We remember tales of the harem. The truth is that Istanbul has no glory except its situation. It is a city of steep, cobbled, noisy hills. Taxis and buses fling the human body about at sudden corners; the distances are long and exhausting. The chief hotels are in the European quarter, called Beyoğlu. It has improved its appearance in recent years, but it is still heavy, rather

Germanic, and ugly. One's constant idea is to get out of it.

You make your way to the Galata Bridge, cross the Golden Horn to the heart of the old city, and meet the Turkish swarm head on. Aesthetes detest the bridge, but, for myself, the swarm and the noise are the making of it. There is the merchant shipping on the Golden Horn; the blasting of the scores of smoking ferries; the mess of fishing boats, barges, tugs, and wherries along the quays, and on every barge dozens of people dropping lines into the dirty water and bringing up fish at the rate of two a minute.

The rush hour in Naples cannot compare with the Galata crowds. With thick black hair, thick black eyebrows, and scowling, too, they cross the long bridge eight deep, the ragged and the elegant. You are bawled at by old porters bent double under fearful loads. They are carrying huge pieces of furniture, yards of steel, cases of glass, hundredweights of cloth. With a carrying frame or leather hump on their backs, they are the pack mules of the city, unable to see where they are going, but shouting their way forward at a fast pace. Soon they will be climbing hills that rise at a gradient of one in four. In doorways everywhere you see these men, with their ropes on their knees, waiting for the next job. And yet, in this gruff, solemn crowd, I have seen a man walk dreamily across the bridge, treading with the delicacy of a young pasha, leading a beautifully brushed white Angora goat with a red silk bow on its neck.

Dust and smoke are in your eyes, the curious smell of Istanbul is in your nostrils, something compounded, it seems, of hair oil, nougat, and spice. You make your way past the enormous grey mosque at the foot of the bridge.

Mosques of this size have the air of squatting froglike on the ground. They stare at you like globular faces. You pass a wall where the public letter writers are sitting, sad, chain-smoking, cynical men. One is tapping with two fingers at his old typewriter while a customer stands by, anxiously telling him what to say. You fight your way through the traffic to the spice market, which is mainly a stretch of passages under stone arches. You are engulfed in the smells of spices, most of which you cannot name. Stranger still, people are buying them.

At the entrance to the market, and up a hidden staircase, is one of the best restaurants in Istanbul, run by a Greek whose original place was wrecked during the savage anti-Greek riots of 1955. It takes a lot to discourage the tenacious Greek, whose people were in Turkey long before the Ottoman Empire.

Beyond the spice market is the street market, which resembles an Arab *souk*. Mostly the shops sell cloth, clothes, stockings, shoes, the Greek traders rushing out, with cloth unrolled, at any potential customer, the Turks passively waiting. Porters shout; everyone shouts; you are butted by horses, knocked sideways by loads of bedding, and, through all this, you see one of the miraculous sights of Turkey—a demure youth carrying a brass tray suspended on three chains, and in the exact centre of the tray a small glass of red tea. He never spills it; he manoeuvres it through chaos to his boss, who is sitting on the doorstep of his shop.

One realizes there are two breeds in Turkey: those who carry and those who sit. No one sits quite so relaxedly,

188

expertly, beatifically as a Turk; he sits with every inch of his body; his very face sits. He sits as if he inherited the art from generations of sultans in the palace above Seraglio Point. Nothing he likes better than to invite you to sit with him in his shop or in his office with half a dozen other sitters: a few polite inquiries about your age, your marriage, the sex of your children, the number of your relations, and where and how you live, and then, like the other sitters, you clear your throat with a hawk that surpasses anything heard in Lisbon, New York, or Sheffield, and join the general silence.

Not all sitters are pleasant to look at. In Istanbul, as in many Turkish towns, there is a horrible population of half men—the legless, the paralyzed, the withered—who sit in their wheeled trays. The East conceals nothing, and you are astounded to see how many of these creatures are handsome, domineering, and lordly, and how they look contemptuously at your legs as you pass.

Now you come to the Grand Bazaar, the enormous, arched city-within-a-city of shops. You wander under the white arches, in an area that is really three or four large department stores spread out on the single floor of a labyrinthine cave. Here is the alley of the carpet dealers, here of coppersmiths, here of furniture, jewelry, silks. You buy anything from leather for your shoes to pianos, from a ring to a bedroom suite. The scene can be matched in Cairo or in the cities of India, but here it has turned drab since 1922, when Kemal Atatürk ordered Turkey to be Western, though it is still fantastic to the Western eye.

Only beyond the Bazaar, on the promontory where the

palace of the sultans stands with the domes of Sancta Sophia and the Blue Mosque, do you recover something of the magnificence of the city. Here you stand before one of the most beautiful skylines in the world. Sunrise or, best of all, sunset is the time to see it, especially from the hills of the Golden Horn or from the sea. Then the steel-grey domes become black cut-outs against the sky and the delicate minarets prick it like daggers. One might be looking at some magical city floating on a carpet in the air, a place voluptuous, brilliant in design, and with a beauty that is cruel and vacant. To obtain precisely this effect of a dome floating free in the air without noticeable support was the ambition of the builders of the mosques; and inside them the illusion is triumphant.

Other Turkish creations are the exquisite kiosks, or summerhouses, in the palace. They are the work of a virile race at the peak of its civilization, but also in all the sumptuousness of its decadence. And the towered walls of old Istanbul encircle the palace ruinously. Earthquakes rather than sieges have cracked the towers and sent down tons of their masonry, but the remains stand massively in decay for miles, and they remind one of the Ottoman power. Now, in the crannies, are the slums and Gypsy camps of the city.

Many travellers have found in Istanbul the stagnant melancholy of cities long past their great period. The modern Turk has little regard for the past. He has pulled down whole quarters recklessly in a fever to spend money and be modern at all costs. Istanbul, like other European cities, is being hacked to pieces by speculators in land and property. But the situation of Istanbul is indestructible.

The little towns and harbours of the Bosporus are prim but pretty; and exiles from the city talk with affection of past summers spent on the Princes Islands in the Sea of Marmara about twelve miles from the Golden Horn, swimming off lazy beaches in the white heat haze.

When the air is leaden on the mainland, you can refresh yourself by going over to the islands. On weekends the ferries are crowded with families who, if they are rich, are going to their island villas. These are in the extraordinary and traditional style of Turkish timber building, strange fretwork places, carved in every inch, and they stand in scented gardens cut out of the scented scrub.

On these islands there is a silence one had entirely forgotten. No cars are allowed there; there is no gasoline anyway. Some of the trippers hire a horse carriage and trot up to the pine woods to picnic on the hot promontories that go violently down to the sea. Others stay in the sultry little ports and eat at the restaurants on the quays. They eat the excellent fish that comes down the Bosporus from the Black Sea, and mussels fried and served cold, in their shells, with rice and raisins. Drinking water has to be brought from the mainland. There is good strong beer everywhere in Turkey, and drinkable light wine; but the mass of people drink fruit juice, goat's milk, or water.

After their meal they make for the pastry shop "for something sweet." The Turkish craving, not to say greed, for sweet things—nougats, marzipans, Turkish delight, almond pastes, and sweet creams—is not inhibited by any regard for the figure; both sexes are delighted by *embonpoint* and contented chins. In any case, the sugar is a source of energy in a climate that constantly saps it. One of the island sights in autumn, when the season is over, is the rows of refrigerators on the quays. The rich are taking them back to their houses in Istanbul. They will be loaded onto some strong man's back.

To understand the basic conflict in Turkish life and probe into the dilemmas of Westernization, one has to cross the Bosporus and take the plane or the night train to Ankara, the modern capital—and afterwards visit the real Turkey, the long, burned-up stretches of the Anatolian steppe and the primitive mud-walled villages and little towns of the interior. In this region of treeless distance and arid mountain, Kemal Atatürk arbitrarily placed his capital after the First World War. He chose a deep, wide valley where water could be brought, and there he planted a modern German-style city of wide boulevards and pleasant suburban streets.

Under Atatürk the Caliphate was abolished. Religion came under control of the State. The Latin script replaced the Turkish or Arabic. The powerful Moslem sects and secret societies, such as the dervishes of Konya, were dissolved. The story has often been told of how Atatürk banned the wearing of the fez and threw his own fez to the ground. Much excitement was caused in the outside world when he made the wearing of the veil illegal, but the continuous wars had already done something to emancipate Turkish women, and the formal veil, strictly worn, was a town fashion rarely adopted by peasant women who worked beside the men in the fields.

Atatürk's policy of making Turkey Western and of industrializing the country by drastic and expensive State planning has been followed by every Turkish government since his death in 1938. A very large part of Turkish industry is organized by the State, and Turks often say to Westerners: "We have had socialism before the rest of you. Why should we want a socialist party?" Most of educated Turkey supports this policy, and the nation today is fundamentally the work of intellectuals and technicians supported by the army. The educated also support Kemal's wish that Turkey should become a typical parliamentary democracy with a party system.

And I remember a distinguished and very formal old gentleman, a connoisseur of *objets d'art,* who showed me the treasures of the "Turkish corner" of his lovely modern house—the long pincers that had held the charcoal for lighting a sultan's cigarette, his lovely embroideries from the fifteenth century, his golden chalices, the little throne of cushions on which the master of the house had sat cross-legged. He translated the Arab proverbs that were framed on the walls of his salon, those large, sweeping, elegant pieces of Arabic script in black on gold that are much admired in the Middle East. The Turk is addicted to proverbs: "Do not trust the man to whom you have done a favour." Or "Take the straight path; if you wander by devious ways, you may fall into a hole." He quoted one about simplicity: "A coat and a piece of bread suffice."

My connoisseur had been educated at Heidelberg. A considerable number of educated Turks have been taught in Germany, London, Paris, or the United States. I spent

193

much time with a vivacious and successful young playwright who had been to Cornell—the theatre flourishes in Ankara and Istanbul, and many new theatres are being built—and it was he who came out frankly with a statement that a foreigner who has a regard for Turkish sensibilities must be careful not to make. The basis of ordinary Turkish life, he said, was tribal, rather in the tradition of the Welsh. I could not believe my ears when I heard the word "tribal" from a Turk; it is resented because in the remote frontier districts there survive primitive Asiatic nomads, the Kurds, who are slowly being assimilated. He meant the word in the sense of moral inheritance: the tribe traditionally cannot allow opposition; everything must be submitted to discussion until all, not a majority, are of the same mind. If there is one incurable dissentient, he must be thrown out.

"We are Westernizing Turkey," he said, "but in our own way, not yours; we are unlike you. We have had no feudal system. We have no bourgeoisie, no proletariat. What progress we have made has been the work of idealists, intellectuals, and soldiers—hence the strength of their position."

What confronts the Westernized Turks is the gulf between their life in the fine modern flat with the superb view and the primitive life of the steppe. There is almost no link between the two. A few miles outside Ankara, one is back 3,000 years in the mud-walled villages. There the women, dressed in floral-patterned trousers, and nervously drawing their shawls over their faces, sit among children on the roofs of their huts, spinning or making blanket coats for the shepherds for the winter, or squat on the ground cooking, with cow dung for fuel, among the animals they share their life with. They stumble over the boulders of the village street, carrying water on yokes. The goats and cows and chickens and geese wander among them. At night they light their oil lamps.

Hardly a tree is to be seen for tens of miles. The goats nibble the scarce, wiry yellow grass and thistles, and very pretty these animals look, but as they wrench away every growing thing in their teeth, they make it more certain that soil erosion—the great curse of Turkish agriculture—will be worse the following year. You are looking at a landscape of stone; and over the rough road the white dust clouds hang for a quarter of a mile behind the passing lorry, obliterating the peasant as he trots on his donkey. There are perhaps 40,000 villages in Turkey, scattered and almost invisible until you come to them on the plain. And often no mosque marks the spot. In one of those mud villages outside Ankara, the State has built an agricultural college —it even has a Greek theatre—and a model settlement ready for occupation. An excellent, exemplary idea—but the wretched peasants cannot possibly afford the rents that will be demanded.

You travel about Anatolia by plane or by the local bus. I took the bus to Konya, a thriving town of over 100,000 inhabitants—a bone-shattering journey of 170 miles. At half past five in the freezing morning of the steppe, the bus station at Ankara is packed like a fair. You get a glass of hot goat's milk from the cauldrons that stand on fires in the open; you buy one or two hard bread rolls—very good

—for the journey, and so bang and rattle away. When the radio is turned off, couples quietly sing to each other.

The open landscape impresses with empty distances, clear sky, far-off mountains as pale as gas, the land grey or straw-coloured in the fierce sun, and at sunset the mountains sharpening to violet, the plain turning to pink and then lavender, the sky clear green. At night the stars appear nearly to touch the earth.

The day on the steppe is unforgettable in its spaciousness and austerity. The only living things for miles, for hours at a time, are the herds of white or black goats. The only man-made objects are the tall crosstrees at the wells, each with a bucket hanging from the end of a pole twenty feet long; and the occasional circles of jagged stone by the side of the road, sticking up a foot or two at random angles from the ground, like rotten teeth. These patches of stone are village burying grounds, the most neglected, naked cemeteries I have ever seen. No sheltering walls surround them. The dead are out on the dusty steppe as they were in life.

Several of the women in our bus wore the traditional non-Western dress—the long blue cotton coat worn over baggy red, blue, or green cotton trousers, and the white, flowing headdresses under which they could half hide their faces. Moslem habit—and the desire to protect the complexion—hangs on here. When we stopped, the women would get out and at once squat in the road directly behind the bus and wait there until someone gave them a push with his foot to get them up and into the bus again. In Konya itself—an important and thriving market town with fine new factories on the outskirts—half the women wore

Western dress, but there were wonderfully beautiful and elegant women wearing a sort of low turban of twisted black-and-white cloth, the white veil up to the mouth, golden embroidered coats, and brilliant baggy red trousers bound at the waist by vivid bands of green and blue.

Konya has a modern boulevard and government buildings. It has a modern café or two, a cinema, some villas on the outskirts, and three modern hotels. It tries to be Western. You can buy paperbacks there; the Turks, unlike the clever Greeks, *do* read. Konya has the mosque of the whirling dervishes, a thirteenth-century sect of mystics, now suppressed. The dervishes are allowed to perform their ritual dance only in one week in December of each year, although one hears that this highly political sect still flourishes underground. This particular mosque is now, like Sancta Sophia in Istanbul, a museum.

The silence of mosques is different from the silence of churches. It is the soft silence of the living room. You take off your shoes at the door and enter what might be a luxurious drawing room. The prayer carpets appear to blaze like red ground flame, a floor on fire. And when, as in the mosque of the dervishes, you look at the long, sloping tombs of the founder of the order and his kin, who lie under gorgeous embroideries, each with a large, startling turban wound round the phallic stump at the head, death seems disturbingly alive. These figures, one would say, still rule. Perhaps, secretly, they do. The effect is all the more macabre because the tombs are aboveground, furnished and apparelled. One can imagine the dead throwing aside the trappings of the tomb and rising up to speak.

Konya is a small provincial capital, typical of the plain.

Once famous and the seat of sultans, it is now a market town dealing in grain and horses. The peasants drive in with their prettily painted horse carts, in which the grain is heaped loose, and pitch it on the floors of the dealers' sheds. The millstones grind. Scores of stinking, rickety horse cabs go through the streets; no one walks far if he can help it. The whole hot town smells of spice and horse dung. In the large backyards the country people sit on their bundles, their faces blackened by the sun, watching the dealers walk the horses around.

In Konya's bazaar quarter the streets split up into trades. Here the coppersmiths and tinsmiths are beating out cauldrons three feet wide. Here are the rope makers, the carpenters, and—very important in Turkey—the makers of hard cushions and low divans, like floral car seats, for in Anatolia the peasant sits and sleeps close to the floor. They put their babies to sleep in hammocks. The activity of the streets is frantic; the smells are violent. The cripples and beggars rage from their place in the dust by the walls. The bus station is crowded with men, women, and children, loaded with enough baggage to take them across the world; all bus journeys are long in this empty country. In a quiet mosque you see the men sitting cross-legged in prayer. Outside, men and women are washing their arms, their hands, their feet, before going in. Food is simmering in large pans at the windows of the eatinghouses or roasting in great stone ovens under blazing fires.

The foreigner need never be alone in Turkey. When I got off the bus in Konya, I was stupefied by the crowd. Three or four poor men came up at once to help, but I could not make myself understood. Then a young man

with a few words of French came along. He attached himself to me, not as a guide or tout, but as a friend. We hired
a cab; we ate fruit together, visited mosques. I noticed that,
in good Moslem fashion, he always gave a coin to a beggar.
Who he was, what he was, I cannot say; his French was
not equal to it, but we were friends who gazed at each
other like a pair of speechless animals.

He would not leave me until he handed me over to an
English-speaking family who were on a visit from Ankara
and who at once took charge of me. The father was one
more Turkish economist—he spends half the year in Wash-
ington and has great scorn for Western hotels, restaurants,
and food. The best food in Konya, he said, was in the
reeking little eatinghouses, so we went around them while
he shouted in at the doorways to ask what meat they had,
and could he see it. We settled on a dirty, fly-infested
place where he approved of the lamb. He picked out the
best pieces for us, and it was excellent. It was served to us
in an upper room under a great pile of those thick, spongy,
flavourless pancakes you meet everywhere from Istanbul
to Delhi, and eventually get a taste for, and we washed it
all down with glasses of goat's milk. The other customers
were thin, ragged, ravenous workmen who tore at their
food with their hands.

Often the Turks of the steppe seemed to me like the
Spaniards of Castile, though without the pride and fantasy.
The landscape is Castilian. Anyone who has travelled
through the fantastic stretch of lunar pinnacles north of
Almería in Spain, and seen the troglodyte dwellings in
Guadix, will respond to the mad, whitish, ghostly landscape
of eroded rock southwest of Kayseri in Anatolia. The

town lies northeast of Konya. Here the rock is whirled into chimneys, tents, even human shapes. It is holed by caves which have been turned into dwellings—and even into churches, many with remarkable Byzantine frescoes.

From Ankara I flew to Antalya on the Mediterranean coast, southwest of Konya. It is a flight over the high peaks that shut off the tableland, a flight from sunny autumn to blue, blazing sea and torrid summer. The pine forests begin on the sandy lower slopes; and the sand turns to bright orange where it meets the emerald shallows of the sea. The plane bumps down in a cloud of dust. Antalya is locked into a deep gulf by immense mountains and a peak of snow. It is a fishing port mounted on high red cliffs that look like rotting cheese; you see the water frilling around the rocks below, but never hear it. Rich Turks keep villas in Antalya and leave their wives there with the children. It is a lazy, dusty little subtropical town, shaded by palms in the main streets, by fig trees in the gardens, refreshed by innumerable streams and waterfalls.

The roads of Antalya, hedged by oleanders and tall cane, run out into a rich coastal plain of cotton fields, green rivers, and Classical ruins. At Perga and Side, nearby, earthquakes have tumbled the enormous masonry of the Greek theatres and the Roman hippodromes, but at Aspendos I found the largest and most complete ancient theatre I have ever seen. Somehow it has escaped catastrophe. You stand inside it at noonday in the silence of eighteen centuries. Only a lizard or a snake slips across the stone seats where an audience once sat.

All this coast is rich in relics of Greek and Roman

colonization. Where a civilization once was, there are now thistles and tumbled columns, and the goatherd stands with his tinkling flock. You pass through the dusty villages. The brown pack camels slop along the roads, the donkeys trot, the lorries bulge with bales of cotton, the pickers are in the fields, the wagtails flicker in the roads, the snow-fed rivers run smoothly green. At Side you sit under the thatched awning of the rough tavern by the lapping sea, driving off the flies and the starving cats while you eat fish and the eternal Turkish salad of cucumber, tomato, and peppers and drink your goat's milk and water. Brown youths swim in the bay, and parties of Turkish schoolmasters and schoolmistresses come to the tavern and unpack their luncheons of cold chops, rice, and fried eggplant spread with yogurt.

The sun has eaten into everything and everyone, fading the patched country clothes, so that poverty itself is simply an aspect of the heat. Although the place where you have eaten is neglected and dirty, you are glad to be out of the sun. You notice that the Turks, after they have eaten, go, like all good Moslems, to wash their faces and hands at the fountain nearby. Your driver, now that he is idle, has taken out his beads to play with—the "nervous beads" that you see in every man's hands throughout Greece, Asia Minor, and India. This is one of the most sensible and simple forms of therapy, invented by peoples who have mastered the art of total relaxation of the body. They know how to sit and soothe the restlessness of the idle, itching hand.

In its older parts, Antalya is a town where the side

streets are as rough as headlong riverbeds. The lower parts
of the houses are of stone, the upper parts of carved wood,
overhanging. The women sit on cushions or pretty mat-
tresses on the floor. At dusk the people leave the cotton
fields; the camels are put out to graze. You see the mountains go red and then violet and finally to the bloom of
blackness, as the sun goes down and the crowds are in the
street. Mustapha, Ahmed, Suleiman—the women shout for
their children.

Anyone you pass in the street is certain to be quietly
singing to himself one of those endless, ululating, wailing
Turkish songs that sound like the choking tears and gut-
tural cries of pleasure. One woman is murmuring these
songs to another woman as they walk, and men to men, as
if these pillow sighings and erotic whimperings were all
they thought of. A dozen businessmen at dinner, sitting
under the thick trees and looking down at the moonstruck
water of the gulf, stopped eating while each in turn sang
one of these quivering, pleading Eastern songs which have
hardly any words. All had this extraordinary art of using
their vocal cords as if they were plucking at strings.

The Turks are glad to chatter to the stranger in bits
of French, English, and, occasionally, German. Whether
they are college students, hotel servants, waiters, whether
they are training for engineering, medicine, the civil service, or doing any job that comes along, these young men
with the large girlish eyes are united in one thing: they
want to be soldiers. "My father and my grandfather were
killed in the Yemen. I want to die like them," said a modest
young boxer. The military life for them! They despise the

occupations they will eventually have to take up. Among the young men of the world, they alone are eager for their military service.

Along the Russian frontier, they like to boast, it is usually the Turkish peasant who provokes the incidents. Their favourite sport along the northeastern frontier is to step over into Russia and chop down a tree. The peasants are terrible destroyers of trees, and the State has a hard time stopping them. There are notices in the forests saying: "Do not kill these trees. They are your life," and in theory the death penalty exists for the axe-happy. (The urban Turk delights in trees, as one can see in the oasis he has planted in Ankara.)

The young Turk not only admires the military tradition but also argues back hard if you criticize it. They admire their left-wing army. In Antalya, people were preparing to celebrate the founding of the Republic, and I saw the actual celebration far up on the Aegean coast, in Izmir (Smyrna). The high-school girls in their black smocks and black stockings, the youths, and the crack regiments made a fine sight on the march, not at all Germanic, not at all machinelike in the Iron Curtain way, but with a natural grace. And they carried a huge picture of Atatürk. He was a soldier, and he liberated them.

There are countries that are all over in a flash from the traveller's point of view. Turkey is one that can become an addiction, especially for those who are excited by noble landscapes. The coasts are as stupendous here as in Greece, and the traveller who goes by steamer from Antalya or

Izmir around to Istanbul will have something that complements his Greek experience. Izmir was, of course, a Greek city until 1922, and the dramatic ancient sites of Ephesus and Bergama—the new name for Pergamum—are nearby. Although a great part of Izmir was destroyed in the Greco-Turkish war, and although the majority of its Greek population has gone, it is still a lively port. The ships come to the quays in the heart of the city; the heavy, curving, green, red, and blue hulls of the sailing luggers rock against the harbour walls. All day the cranes rattle outside your hotel, loading the bales of cotton and the cases of currants. Hundreds of men and boys are fishing off the splendid waterfront.

Turkey is a masculine country, and it is no paradox to add that, although the men seem to be out on the streets all day and half the night, the intense life of the people takes place in the home. Whatever is said about the emancipation of Turkish women, the Moslem tradition goes deep and crumbles slowly and with difficulty. The only public displays of affection are between men: a characteristic sight at evening is the men walking arm in arm in silence and the women together in the same way, with little public interest between the sexes. That is kept severely private.

The cafés are filled with men; women never enter them. There the men sit playing backgammon or talking; more often they sit silently before a glass of water or smoking their hubble-bubble pipes. Occasionally a waiter comes out and places a new piece of charcoal in the little tray at the top of the apparatus; occasionally the smoker, gripping the red or green plush holder of the tube, raises the tip to his mouth like someone playing a note or two on silent bagpipes. In the glass jar at his feet, the water bubbles and the blue smoke clouds. It is all a long, contented protest against time.

At night they will leave and walk up and down in threes and fours, groups of men passing groups of men. Only once did I hear loud talk; a dignified drunk was reciting poetry. At the end he was ironically but decorously applauded by a group of students who paused to listen and then strolled on. Soon the streets were empty. All had gone home, for that is where they like to be. They are said to be uxorious husbands. After all, their courtships have been prolonged and strictly controlled, with a severe eye to the proprieties. They are family men.

And if one asks what is going on in the minds of these family men who are living in a poor, anxious, puritan country that is being violently wrenched by the strong arm of the modern world, the answer perhaps lies in one of the tales of Nasreddin Hodja, the ancient homespun philosopher and Sancho Panza of Turkish folklore. Every man, woman, and child in Turkey loves to quote his droll sayings.

Once (the tale goes) the Hodja dreamed that he was eating a plate of delicious soup, when a neighbour woke him up, saying: "My mother is ill and she asks whether you could give her some soup—if you have cooked any today."

"What fine noses people have," the Hodja said. "They can even smell my dreams."

The modern Turk is caught between delightful dreams of steel mills, sugar refineries, and the seductions of the Common Market—and the soldier's rough awakening.

IRAN

At night, when the plane jumps eastward out of Beirut or Istanbul and sets its nose into Asia, something more than the usual airplane loneliness settles in the mind of the traveller. He feels his Western roots have been torn up. He is heading for emptier spaces, looking down on invisible tribes and turbans, on dust and rock, and on towns half concrete, half mud. If he sees Baghdad lying like a bracelet below or catches sight of the Tigris worming its way painfully toward the yellow flares of the oil wells, the loneliness deepens. Europe is concentrated and intense. Its civilization, ever since the Greeks, has rejected the word "relax." But now the traveller is moving into the world of wide-open areas and thin populations, where despotism is second nature, where the two extremes of violence and passivity are as natural as rock and plain, where freedom is a foreign word. And then he comes down in Tehran and finds he is only half right, and that Iran is strange to him, but not totally strange. He has really come down on an island. Iran may be rather Russian; it may be Asiatic; in fact it is an island in the land ocean of Asia.

I am not talking about the brash pride that a city like Tehran takes in its modernity. The airport is just about the finest I have ever seen. It has cost somebody millions; the place is splendid without being splendacious. The drive into the city, down a fine avenue named Elizabeth II in a fit of enthusiasm, is a floodlit rat race of pelting, swerving, interweaving foreign cars, French, American, British, Russian, and German. The red double-decker buses have been imported from London. The neon signs signal the soft-drink war between Pepsi-Cola, Alpine, and Canada Dry. The traffic in Tehran is mad but inspired; the city looks as if one half is being put up and the other being pulled down, and that it will all be twice as modern by the end of the month. You feel you will be lucky not to be in the hospital by then, after going through a windshield or breaking your leg in some hole in the pavement.

It is not the modernity of Tehran or of any other place in Iran that calms the traveller; it is something else, which the Persians exaggerate but which has an element of truth. They are to some extent a *racial* island. The old name they have revived indicates it: Iran means "land of the Aryans." Their language is Indo-European like our own. Often one hears the echo of a European word. And, although Arab, Mongol, Slavonic, and Turkish blood is in them, they are linked with us through the ancient Greeks. They look at their neighbours, the Iraqis and the Turks, and feel they have more in common with us but have been cut off in the course of the great migrations and invasions of history. This is not altogether an illusion. For three thousand years the Persians have been, before anything else, a cultivated race. They are conscious of being the heirs of a world empire, and of the grace, distinction, and tolerance of old cultures.

Still, even as one feels the undercurrent of a natural affinity in Iran—an affinity one does not feel in the Arab countries—one senses the bewilderment of a double life, Western one moment, Oriental the next. "I wanna tell you," says the elegant young Persian businessman who has spent a year in the United States, "I'm gonna make a million dollars and I'm gonna spend it. I'll give it away." He drives suicidally in his Cadillac. One minute he is telling you how he bribes the Iranian customs to let his machinery in or about the gang war his truck drivers are engaged in; the next he is reciting verses from the fourteenth-century poet Hafiz. Pretty well all Persians can recite Hafiz.

The businessman's father and his family had been merchants who sat cross-legged on their carpets in the bazaar. A brash fellow? Hardly. He is a dandy, speaks three European languages, and in spite of the showing off, is touching in his serious desire to find a friend. His excitability may be due to the altitude: most of Persia is set up on a high tableland, four to five thousand feet up. But there is something besides dizziness in him. In the immediacy of Persian friendship there is something searching, a quest for something indefinable; at heart, every Persian is a mystic. He seeks some absolute *Friend*. This young money hunter was, in fact—as I discovered from many intimate conversations with him—in a state of emotion about the meaning of life, the fascination and uselessness of Fortune. I would not be surprised to hear one day that he had renounced the world and gone into a retreat with the dervishes.

One Friday—the Moslem Sunday—I was taken to a family party at the country house of some rich people. They lived in the hills above Tehran, where the mountains suddenly start up. These bare, snow-covered ranges dominate the city; on the shady side of the streets you feel the whisper of snow on your neck in the spring. The house stood on a little gorge behind a veil of poplars, and from it one looked across a wide, austere panorama of rock and almost treeless wilderness. I was accompanied by the mother and pretty daughter of the Persian family with whom I was living in Tehran, and I was the only man in the party. We went upstairs to the sitting room, taking our shoes off before we went in, for Persians value their carpets highly. I was astonished to see several ladies and their children lying in what appeared to be an enormous bed at one end of the room. I thought at first they were ill.

"Come on," they cried. "Get into bed," and into "bed" we got.

It was not a bed, of course. It turned out to be a large low table, and under it was a charcoal brazier. The table was concealed first by a quilt; on top of that was a large, crisp white sheet; over that was a large carpet. Around the table were bolsters and cushions. We tucked ourselves

in, drew sheet and carpet to our waists, and passed the
rest of the day lolling in the warmth while the servants
brought us sweetmeats, fruits, glasses of tea, and cigarettes.

This was a rich family who preferred to live in the
traditional Persian manner. Yet they were Europeanized
and "advanced"; all except one had been educated in France
or England. They did not wear the *chadar*, or cotton gown,
that serves also as a half-veil.

"What have you noticed in Persia?" they asked.

"You all have beautiful eyes," I said.

"Oh yes, we all have large, gazelle-like eyes," they said.
"Everyone in Persia has. And long noses," they added. "One
of our friends has gone to London to have her nose
altered. Her English is not very good. She wants what she
calls a 'snob nose.' "

"I am told by a French biochemist at the University that
he finds Persian students more intelligent than those he has
taught in any other country," I said.

"Yes," they said. "It is not boasting. We have beautiful
eyes and we are exceptionally intelligent, indeed too intelligent. Each of us is on his own and cannot co-operate with
the others—you see that in the state of the country. Everyone is mad for himself."

Intelligence, intense curiosity, hospitality, courtesy, eager
friendship, great tolerance—these indeed are the virtues of
the country. But, these ladies said, these qualities had
grown out of a long history of foreign conquest. The
conquered Persians had developed all the arts that would
seduce the conqueror; the passion for foreign things, for
assimilating foreign ideas, has enriched the Persian, but

has perhaps made him too *serviable*, a smatterer, his whole intelligence bent on absorbing, not creating. His intelligence has enabled him to be showy and idle; his tolerance has made him passive; his talent for friendship makes him put his obligations to his friends before his obligations to the community.

If the Persian sees himself as an islander in a land ocean, he knows also that Iran is and always has been something else—an open road, and a very wide one. Iran is about the size of the United States east of the Mississippi. It hangs from the Caucasus and the green, forested mountains of the long Russian frontier that runs, interrupted by the Caspian Sea, for much more than a thousand miles across the north. The Caspian is the largest inland body of water in the world, and four fifths of it is a Russian sea. The narrow green coastal strip is a warm, moist region of orange groves and olives, tea gardens, and the flooded rice fields that turn blood red at sunset and have the effect of stained glass. High snow peaks, rising to 18,000 feet, cut this region off from the interior and the south, where the tableland begins, stretching for hundreds of miles to Russia and Afghanistan on the east and on the west to the short frontier with Turkey and the fertile plains of Iraq. But the plateau is not flat. Again tremendous mountains break it up as one travels south to the sands of the Persian Gulf and the oil country, and east to the Himalayas in Pakistan and the true tropic of the Arabian Sea. Saudi Arabia is across the Gulf.

Such is the Iranian road—rough and torrid in summer, freezing in winter, a road throughout history and still a road in the present, wide open to invasion. By this road the

Allies forced the Iranians to let the supplies pass through to Russia during the last war. By this road the Russians infiltrated their agents of revolution after the war and the British pressed up from the south, as they had always done, to defend first India and then their oil interests. Iran is not, for the moment, a military road. In the background, it is controlled by the money of the World Bank, American dollars, the international—and also Iranian—oil interests.

Fourteen hundred miles of open frontier with the Soviet Union, a feudal economy built on the backs of poor peasants, and the traditional hatred of Russia present the Iranians with a difficult dilemma. They have, however, always been in this situation. It has become sharper since Iraq withdrew from the Baghdad Pact. The only answer they see is rapid Westernization—dam building, modernizing of agriculture, industrialization, social reform; they rush into this hoping somehow to escape, on the one hand, violent social revolution and possible invasion and, on the other, bankruptcy. The old feudal order and its habits are very tenacious. The Shah refuses merely to reign; he rules. His popularity is uncertain. He has given away his own land. He is trying to break up the big estates; and although his program was endorsed heavily by a referendum, he has a tricky time steering a course between the old order, with its powerful family interests, and the young unemployed intellectuals, who have been created by Westernization. I met few of the younger generation who think the next decades will be peaceful.

The single uniting force—and in a crisis it overrules— is nationalism, or rather, since no Nasser has appeared, pride in the Iranian tradition. "We are an ancient race who have had a great culture; now we must make a civilization" —how often I have heard that said. The Greeks—their opposite numbers in Europe—say the same; and all one can say is that of all the Middle Eastern peoples, the Iranians speak in a voice that is closest to our own in the West— maybe misleadingly so. Under the polish, the boundless hospitality and natural courtesy, under the subtlety, the cleverness, the rapid power of assimilation, is something tough, obstinate, explosive, and headlong. Their oil makes them rich, and if the wealth could be kept out of the fortune hunter's private pocket and honestly and ably managed, they would succeed in creating a stable modern society.

Tehran is the home of the Westernizing movement in Iran, the movement begun by Riza Shah, the father of the present Shah, after 1921. Riza Shah was a young officer in the Persian cossacks who threw out the old feudal regime, acting very much in the manner of Kemal Atatürk in Turkey: he abolished the political and juridical privileges of the foreign communities—British, French, Russian, and German, the so-called "capitulations"—saw to the building of the first railway, opened mosques to non-Moslems, broke the power of the mullahs, or "teachers of the sacred law," forbade the wearing of the veil. The enormous British and Russian embassies standing opposite each other like fortified citadels in the middle of Tehran are reminders of foreign dominance during the Victorian age. Sanctuary is a traditional resort in times of political unrest—nowadays all Persian politicians are considered to be "untouchable" in the telegraph offices!—and in one of the crises of the nineteenth century, 20,000 Persians took refuge in the enormous grounds of the British embassy.

In Turkey, Atatürk proclaimed a republic; but Riza Shah mounted what has always been called the Peacock Throne. This is not a figure of speech: the throne can be seen in the Golestan Palace, jewelled and shimmering. The palace is a tiled confection glittering with glass mosaic, and its floors are covered with immensely valuable Persian carpets. To connoisseurs of what Théophile Gautier called *l'ennui royal*, Golestan, with its huge collection of the awful presents royalty give to each other, is a startling example of Oriental hodgepodge. The courtesies of power politics fossilize rapidly, and royal taste was running down fast in the nineteenth century.

There are one or two pleasant buildings in neo-Persian style in Tehran; but for the rest, it has deeply shaded avenues which half conceal an architecture that is a jumble of American, German, the Boulevard Raspail, and *Ben Hur*. The general colour is the pale yellow or pink of dusty brick, and the city is, in the main, built low. From the plain outside, all you can see are the dozens of tall chimneys of the outlying brick fields. The native Persian things in Tehran—apart from the bazaar, which is not as interesting as the bazaars of Isfahan and Shiraz—are the small houses.

I am writing this in one of them. You go down a side lane, avoiding the metal rings on the sewage traps in the middle, and knock at a closed door. A tiny servant girl, aged twelve, rushes to you, kisses both your hands, and leads you across a small, tiled courtyard in which young apricot and cherry trees are flowering. In the middle is a pool of turquoise-blue tiles with goldfish in it and a little fountain. The house is a yellow brick box three stories high. There are tens of thousands of little houses in Tehran like this one, and all the charm of Persia is in their carpeted quiet and in the flowering courtyards. There people sit, there the neighbours come—people are always in and out of one another's houses and lives, for they delight in inquisitive friendship—there the continual glasses of tea are brought. Every time I go down to telephone, the child brings me a glass of tea or I am offered something sweet to eat. In a downstairs room, another servant, an old woman in a spotted *chadar*, is sitting cross-legged on the floor ironing, surrounded by gossips. There is, thank heaven, no radio or television. If I want these, I go around to another house like this one, to one of the Prime Minister's secretaries: he has both and turns them on together—and he drinks whiskey!

Life in Tehran has this easygoing gregariousness. At night you go for walks, go to see the wrestlers, or visit the Zur Khaneh, the House of Strength, where teams of a dozen men, dressed in embroidered knee-length trousers, dance, stamp, leap into the air holding staves across their shoulders, juggle, and whirl round like spinning tops to the beat of drums. These are virile feats. You sometimes see these masterful acrobats at the popular music hall, the Shekufeh-No, down in the slum quarter of Tehran, where the Arab belly dancers also perform. The Persians go out *en famille*, wife, aunts, children, all together, to see these shows and eat an enormous meal of mutton and rice as they watch. The ladies, I noticed, discreetly look the other

216

way when the Arab belly dancers come on; the traditional Persian dances are much more beautiful in costume and are more spirited.

In Tehran one can forget the dramatic emptiness of the Persian road. One can fly now to most big towns in the country, looking down on the dry, yellow, leathery land ripped across by mountains, or crawl across it by bus. It is difficult to travel alone because all your friends want to come with you or to send you to stay with their relations. I travelled with an official who had been a schoolmaster. He had what I can only describe as a "call" to visit all his in-laws and cousins and the scenes of his past life. He was the son of a mullah—a monogamous mullah too—very senti-mental, affectable, possessive, kind, given to moralizing, stern with beggars, and the hottest bargainer in bazaars I have ever met. He tried to teach me Arabic and Persian at once; grammar delighted him. Every time the bus skidded, he would rise up and harangue the driver and the rest of the passengers as if we were pupils in his class. We quar-relled once, when I refused to inspect some Girl Guides. He was very hurt.

From Tehran we went south to Qum, one of the two fanatical cities in Iran; the other is Meshed, near the Russian frontier. The emptiness begins almost at once. For hours you jolt in a cloud of dust over a dead-straight road that begins well, but is soon rough, flinty, and pot-holed. It is a switchback ride from plain to pass and plain to pass again. Nothing could be more monotonous, and yet, because of the moutain horizon, it is dramatic. The

217

signs of life are few; the telegraph posts marching across the vacant space add to the sense of distance and loneliness. Rarely are there trees, and then they are enclosed in a little mud-walled orchard. Never is there a bush; the only growing things are the tufts of camel grass, and it is astonishing that the flocks of black, heavy-tailed sheep find enough to eat.

It is rare to see a car on the road, and rare, too, to see a human being. There may be a shepherd or two, some nomad in the distance, or the tall blind men in rags whom one would observe two miles away on the brow of a hill, a long staff in one hand and the other held out for alms. In a day's journey, from sunrise to sunset, we saw no more than a dozen. But for me the symbol of the loneliness of the Persian road was a figure who came sadly out of his mud hovel waving a handful of straw at us. "He is signalling that he wants a match to light his fire," the schoolmaster said.

Vast stretches of this tableland are dust bowl. The topsoil has gone; in the winter the surface is a sea of mud. The goats long ago destroyed the trees, as so often in the Middle East, and the sun burns up everything else. Occasionally there is the distant flash of what might be lake water—but it is salt pan. Very often we passed the ruined mud walls of a village that had been abandoned, or of some caravanserai no longer used, or the blue-tiled dome of a small shrine; and if, in some fortunate spot, the ground was cultivated, or a few cherry trees were in flower, it was walled in from the barren land around. Twice an eagle swooped in ragged elegance over our bus. We saw few inhabited villages, but moved from plain and pass into regions of rock that looked like the remains of a fantastic incineration; rock ochred, reddened, whitened, or metallic and cindery, scalloped into strange cones and tors or sliced into bleak and sandy mesas. They are the outcrop of mountains over which glaciers have slid. The jagged mountains of Iran are young and savage.

Hour after hour the bus plugs away at the road before it passes an inhabited village. In these villages the millions of Iran live in the winter snow, the spring mud, and the oven heat of the dry summer. They are surrounded by low mud-and-straw walls built around a large central court where the life of the community goes on. There is a single gateway, and the wall is for defense; until very lately, villages were often raided by the nomad tribes of Iran. Although they look squalid to the eye and the latrines stink, the village houses are clean, and the people are famous for their honesty and fine bearing.

Many of Iran's leaders spring from humble village stock, for Persian society, unlike India's, has never been caste-ridden. In spite of absolute kings and feudal lords, an able villager can rise to great influence. Persian despotism has been oddly democratic. The villagers are sharecroppers under the big landowners, the so-called "1,000 families" who own Iran. I have heard landowners saying things like: "I have three villages there; they bring me rice, corn, silk, tea," according to the region, as if they owned these people. The landowner is not necessarily a remote personage even if he is rich (in general, the system becomes oppressive when the landowner is an absentee and is represented by an agent), and there is more mixing of classes on an intimate human level under this feudal system, and less master-man or impersonal corporation-employee relationship, than in advanced industrial societies. Politically, of course, land-lordism is now violently unpopular. It is economically be-yond the powers of the wealthiest landlord to modernize Iranian agriculture, at any rate in the tableland.

Water is the key to the life of these villages. In vast areas it is not to be had; in others it has to be piped from the snow mountains, often for very long distances. The Ira-nians solved the engineering problem 2,000 years ago by the system called the *qanat*. As you drive along, you see a belt of holes leading like tracks across the plain for miles to the foot of the mountains. These are the ventilation holes of a deep underground water tunnel which must constantly be kept clear by manual labour, and which runs from a shaft in the mountains that may go down 500 or 1,000 feet. It has been cut by hand. This method of water-piping, the Persians say, is unknown in any other land, though one hears of occasional imitations.

The villages of Iran are almost invisible, for they are the colour of the earth. The houses are like boxes, though sometimes the roofs are built in the cupola style and look like settings of duck eggs. The teahouses or inns are far apart, built for need and not for the pleasure of travel. You push aside the carpet that hangs over the door and find yourself in a cobbled and high-raftered, blue-washed hall. Around the walls are what seem to be wide plank beds, railed off, with carpets on them. In a corner are stacked the bedrolls for those who are staying the night.

The rich family in its American car, the poor labourer, and the lorry driver crowd in, take off their shoes, and sit cross-legged on the plank couches. There are also chairs and rough tables.

You go straight to the primitive kitchen, helping your-self to a couple of raw eggs on the way, and ask for your *chelow kebab*, the standard dish. First a huge plate of rice is brought—Persians really know how to cook rice—then a strip of lamb. It is tender, if sweetish in taste, and also lean because the fat of the Persian sheep is concentrated in a large wad at its tail. You chop the meat into the rice, add a slab of sheep's butter, mash in the raw eggs, pour a cup of yogurt on top, season with saffron or red condi-ment, mix the whole lot together, and eat with the help of a spoon and a thin strip of rubbery bread that is essentially an oversized pancake. This bread is excellent, and after a hard journey begun at five or six in the morning, you find your *chelow kebab* excellent, too, though a little monotonous to my taste. The inn is crude, but it has been like that for a thousand years or more.

You can generally get a stewed marrowbone of beef to finish up with and some radishes, tarragon, and parsley for salad, but no dressing. They eat the meat the day the animal is killed. They can generally find a little bottle of Persian vodka, a soft sour-sweet drink, rather sickly, but on the whole Iranians drink little alcohol. Their vodka is very weak stuff compared with the Anglo-Saxon fire-waters.

These rough meals on the road are good. One is told not to eat beef because it is likely to be full of parasites.

In spite of the terrible stories of "Persian tummy" and amoebic dysentery that travellers bring back, I suffered no ill effects. Good Persian cooking is far better than any other in the Middle East, and not as hotly spiced as the Indian.

The inns are always crowded. The women in their *chadars* squat in the courtyard. At one place there was a resident dervish, a holy beggar—there are a good many unholy ones—who lived in a hole in the wall. The old man claimed to be a hundred and twenty years old and squatted on his plank, tending a little charcoal brazier in which two pots of tea were stewing. He whined out a few prayers, gave us a little white sweet to eat, and expected a few coins.

The holy city of Qum is the only town on the road to Isfahan; it is a busy place, out of tune with the general Persian tolerance. The Great Mullah who lived there had lately died, an old man of ninety, and the town was in a state of religious tension, all strangers being sharply watched, for the stranger is ungodly or detestably Christian. The golden dome of Qum's great, greenish, garish mosque—it is the shrine of Fatima—dominates the flat, dusty, angry city. We called at the governor's office to see if he could smuggle me into the mosque, which is forbidden to strangers, but over the usual glasses of tea he said I was too red-faced to pass as a Persian. We were driven off by an angry crowd when we got up on a roof that commanded a view of the mosque's inner courtyard. Hundreds of drearily chanting schoolboys in long trousers were filing into the place. There is a tendency to religious revival in Iran since the father of the present Shah reduced the power of the mullahs thirty-five years ago. Qum was full of these tall, bearded mullahs stalking about indignantly in their brown cloaks.

Bleaker and more desolate the stretches of land became; snow lit up the peaks of the mountains that barred the way every twenty miles or so. And then the lifeless miles began to liven up with strips of green, processions of thin poplars began, there were long ditches of water—and at last the full, fresh green of Isfahan. To the dust-choked traveller, the sight of the green valley and the brown roofs of Isfahan through the curtains of trees is a delight.

"How nice is this city! How nice are those trees! How nice is that cow! How nice is this water!" the schoolmaster cried. The top of his brown, bald head wrinkled with pleasure; his voice, which was usually argumentative and swaggering, softened, giggled, and became even babyish, and this stern man wriggled with pleasure. The Persian tends to be an expressionless man of strong features, but the small delights of life make him crinkle his face with childish happiness.

Isfahan is the heart of the country, a true Iranian (that is to say, Aryan) city. Like all the towns of the desert and tableland, it is an oasis. A wide yellowish river washes around it, streams run across or under the streets; by the roadside, dozens of women and children are washing clothes, plates, knives and spoons, and themselves, too, in the deep and gushing gutter channels. (They do this even in the streets of Tehran.) The Persians speak of a town as a collection of pools, water channels, and gardens shut behind its walls; and although there are public gardens and palace gardens of some pretension, a garden to them is any place where there is a mud wall, a few poplars, a little green, and a little water. There may be grass during the spring, and flowers, too, but spring soon goes. There is rich lyrical poetry in Persian literature, and the garden always comes into it; but for most of the year a garden is simply the shade and the scent of shrubs and trees. The cypress, admired above all for its womanish shape, appears again and again in Persian love poetry.

Isfahan is too conventionally Moslem to allow representations of nature in the mosaics of its mosques, but their coloured domes seem to float like flowers above the low mud walls and flat roofs of the city. I climbed one of the turquoise minarets of the great Masjid-i-Shah mosque—it was like climbing inside the stalk of some tall, alarming plant—and saw that, except for the coloured domes, the city had no skyline. It was as flat as one of those pancakes of Persian bread.

People from other towns—the regional spirit is strong in this country—think Isfahan set in its ways, strict in religion, and glum despite the grace and the nobility of its mosques and the elegance of its palaces and bridges. It is in fact an industrious city, a place of weavers who have the large textile industry of Persia in their hands, of carpet makers and of tens of thousands of craftsmen who are the backbone of the place.

The bazaar of Isfahan brings home to one that outside of, say, 100,000 people, the rest of Persia lives by a very large number of things made by hand. Cheap fabrics come out of the textile factories, but the hand printers squatting on the floors of the bazaars are colouring them; the potters are potting and painting. I doubt if there are many items of machine-made metal kitchenware in Isfahan. The metal workers are hammering all day at elaborate trays, samovars, grills, and stoves. The fingers of children and young girls have worked on the carpets you see; the task is exacting, for even a coarse rug has sixty knots to the square inch; the making of a single rug goes on for months; and wages are very low. All jewelry is handmade. So are hats, shoes, and slippers.

The Persian who buys in the bazaar is exigent. He expects nothing short of perfection; the defects in machine-made things make him angry. My schoolmaster sent two waiters and a boy to protest against a small defect in a cheap imported machine-made tin opener, and the shopkeeper crawled with shame. The Persian is also displeased with foreigners who pay the first price asked, which is often double what would be paid at the end of half an hour's bargaining—in which both parties put on an emotional act that might have come out of *Othello*. "You are choking me! Are you trying to assassinate me?" the schoolmaster said to a dealer in the Isfahan bazaar. His babyish voice had gone.

Isfahan is the home of the artist-craftsman, the makers of miniatures, inlay work, painters of porcelain, and goldsmiths. For all work that is minute they are as fabulous as Leskov's smiths of Tula, in Russia, who shod an invisible flea for one of the tsars. The traditional Persian genius is for the small decorative detail, and it never breaks with the long tradition of design. This has led Westerners to

225

find Persian art delicate but repetitious and monotonous; yet one has only to see some silent youth sitting upright in his master's shop, putting a lily on a vase; or men on the floor of a mosque, cutting the pattern of a tile; or again, girls sitting in the cradle of a carpet loom, slipping in the coloured threads at incredible speed and never making a mistake, to marvel at the skill and the trancelike absorption of their work and lives.

To go from these scenes to the great mosques of Isfahan is to realize that the mosques are the work of the same minute craftsmanship magnified on a vast scale. Hands, not machines, have built these grandiose yet airy blossomings of tile. Unhappily, the Persian style was imported into the bourgeois West during the nineteenth century, when Persian art was the fashion, and commercialized and vulgarized in café and hotel architecture, so that one may be at first repelled. But the mosques of Isfahan were built in the sixteenth century. If the sixteenth century was the glory of Europe, the same century saw the Persian Renaissance under the Safavid dynasty, which created the third Persian empire from Isfahan. The great square, the Maidani-Shah, with its pinkish and yellowish stone and the great rectangles of its mosques and its royal pavilion, stands with the piazzas of the European Renaissance.

This architecture is as luminous as water and as sensuous as light. It is built to be seen in a strong clear light, against brassy sun and hot blue sky, and to relieve the earthen monotone of the plain. Islam is a legalistic faith. Under the dome, the heart does not aspire to heaven, as it may in the Gothic cathedrals; you are enclosed by the moral formulae of the Law. You stand in a place that may be a worldly court; but if you are thinking of the after life, these mosques tell you precisely how it will be housed: in a palatial, mundane habitation.

The great mosques are simulations. Stone is made to look like silk, clay becomes lace or hangs like the honeycomb; tiled walls rising in elevations high and wide may be walls of handwriting, and indeed, in many, the words of the Koran are there in blatant pronouncement. Again, the glaze simulates a tangible sky or water, for the tiles reflect light and seem to flow. In the Sheik of Lotfollah mosque there is a floor of deep turquoise that one fears to walk on because it appears to be a pool; it is strange to feel the hard tile under one's feet. The paradox of the repetitious art of Persian mosaic is that what seems to be monotonously formal, opaque, and mathematical, should convey a total sense of passing transparent illusion. (That, in fact, is the achievement of all abstract art, when it is good.)

When you go outside the Lotfollah, your Persian friend will love to show you that the sun has moved and that now the pale dome is changing from pale blue and pink to the colour of some strong pollen, like the mimosa, and if you have been regarding the architecture as a collection of logical propositions pleasing only to the brain, you will now know that a proposition may glow and have the tenderness of nature. The Persians of the sixteenth century in Isfahan were building out of light itself, taking the turquoise from their sky, the green of the spring trees, the yellow of the sun, the brown of the earth, the black of their sheep, and turning these into solid light.

No matter where the Moslem prays, whether he puts down his mat in the garden, street, or doorstep or by the roadside, that is his convenient holy place for the moment —and a good Moslem should pray five times a day. The common sight in the courtyards is to see the solitary worshipper kneeling and bowing his forehead to the ground where he pleases, regardless of the friends he is with or the passers-by. He is obeying the Law. One is in a land of observances. The rug is his home, the mosque is his living room open to the sky. In the evenings, just before sunset, students from the university will come to the quiet of these spacious courts to read their books as they walk up and down; and in the Chahar Bagh theological school, where a stream, crossing under the boulevard outside, passes through the courtyard, you see the groups of young bearded students, with their brown robes and shaven heads, sitting cross-legged round the mullah who is teaching them.

Stepping over the bodies of the servants sleeping on the floor in the restaurant of our little hotel, we left Isfahan and set off in the dark, at five in the morning, for Shiraz. Now we saw the nomad tribes beginning to get on the move from the south to the northern grazing territories. The mass movement would come later. Once more, a long day on the road. Sometimes a square black tent with donkeys, a pony or two, or a camel marked a resting place where there was water. The nomad men are tall, black-haired, fine-looking, with faces that seem to be carved out of stone. They wear a small, winged-helmet-like hat that makes them look like supermen who have flown down from outer space. Their faces are as dark as walnut. They hunt the gazelle and the lynx, and bring the skins into the cities for sale. They are also charcoal burners. Occasionally they resort to banditry and, up on the Turkish frontier, to local raids and war.

These tribesmen come into the bazaar at Shiraz with their stocky women, who are unveiled and have stained, wind-polished faces that make them look like Gypsies. They wear their dowry of gold coins across their foreheads and are dressed in gauzy shawls and rich layers of fine petticoats and skirts of brilliant green, gold, and red. They adore finery and everything that is fantastic in dress. One sees groups of them marching with their men through the crowds in the bazaar with the nomad's long, intent, loping strides and with the fierce, naïve look of wary people who live out on the plains. The nomads are used to the free life and the rule of their chieftains, the khans. They are virile and unperturbed, but, like the settled peasantry, they are poor. It is the women who do the heavy work while they carry their babies on their backs; they make the rugs and bedding of their tents and all the clothes of the tribe.

Yet the tribes are not a decadent flotsam on the surface of the life of Iran. There are, it is estimated, about four million tribesmen, and only half of that number are relatively settled. Their chieftains are often men of great wealth, with fine houses in the cities. Many have been educated in France or Great Britain. They have been cabinet ministers, figures at the court of the Shahs, and

229

some have made royal marriages. In Shiraz one can see the palace and superb gardens of one of them who now lives in luxury in California, in exile for his part in an armed rising against the central government.

The tribes are mobile nations, in some respects like the American Indian in the old days, but in a higher condition of development and culture at the top. For thirty years or more the Shahs have tried to subdue them and settle them on the land as agriculturists, in the interests of the peace and unity of Iran. The Iranian army failed to conquer them, or at any rate all of them. A peaceful and subtle approach is being tried now. In Shiraz I met young tribesmen and their sons—but not girls: they are required for manual work—who were being trained as teachers or studying modern husbandry. Mobile tent schools and clinics go up to the tribal territories in the intervals between the seasonal migrations. Like most Persians, these men are exceptionally intelligent; few can read or write, but they learn rapidly. Although their free life is fine, and they are suspicious of anything that will alter the lives of their women, they are quick to see their ignorance in stock breeding and planting. They listen with gravity, and their laughter is frank and independent.

"The tribes are on the move," people say. Soon, in three or four weeks—this was in April—the mass migration would begin. We had seen only the first trickle. The government is at pains to keep any two tribes from meeting at the mountain passes that are the key points of the migrations, for their meetings have often been bloody. And at the passes, the chieftain's agent stands counting the sheep, for he collects a head tax on the flock. Landlordism is the great curse of Iranian life, and the chieftains are as exacting toward their people as the landowners are.

We came out of the mountains and dropped in our cloud of dust to the long green valley where Shiraz lies.

"Welcome," said a young student who met us there. "Welcome to what the guidebooks call 'the city of poets and nightingales.'"

"He speaks," said the schoolmaster scornfully, "with a Turkish accent." Yet the young man had written a thesis on Jane Austen! In *Emma*, he told us, there was a disastrous error of taste: the novelist mentioned that Mr. Woodhouse was afraid of catching cold. The poet Hafiz would never have mentioned so low an affliction! As for Shakespeare— a very inferior poet, who was so poor in imagination that he had to borrow his plots. Firdausi never did that!

I met poets, but heard no nightingales in Shiraz, but the orange blossom and the stock blew their fragrance across this lively city. It sparkles among its gardens under the mountains. It is a place of flowers and handsome avenues, already hot in April. It has a radio station, an airport, and one of the finest modern hospitals in Iran—with flat roofs designed to be pools of cooling water in the summer, for the heat is terrible. Instead of *Dracula*, which was being shown at the cinemas all over the country at this time, they were showing that excellent Russian film *The Cranes Are Flying*. I bought a very expensive French tie.

The governor of the province, a house-proud man, took me on a tour of the town's bakeries, proudly pointing out that he had insisted on plants being put in their windows, and that each bakehouse now had a shower installed. It was one way of insuring that the workmen were clean for the breadmaking. Cleanliness and sanitation were his enthusiasms. The water of Shiraz is good and plentiful, and he could not bear to see the women washing their crocks and their clothes in the roadside channels. He had built a public washhouse and a hostel for beggars.

The governor was very much the clever Sorbonne man; his beautiful young wife was educated in France. The mayor of the city had been at London University, the local general was educated at Harrow, and the young doctor in charge of settling and educating the tribes in this region had been at Harvard and at the University of Kansas. The doctor was an elegant young man with a vocation, and he had been sent down from Tehran on one of the most difficult problems that face the Persian government. He was torn between the boredom of provincial life and his interest in his job. Like all educated Iranians, he was also torn between the fact of belonging to the rich upper class, through whom everything is done, and his concern for drastic reform and his fear of revolution.

There is also a less-well-off middle class of small employees and officials who also live in Western style and are becoming a political force. They have pleasant houses, more barely furnished than ours, for they spend all their money on carpets; the life of their women is more restricted than with us, but they are anxious to pass as modern Westerners. The schoolmaster had a teen-age niece at the local high school, and she was like any teen-ager in the rest of the world. Except that she had an ear for the latest Arab, Persian, Turkish, and Pakistani music on the radio, and that under her school dress she wore tight-fitting trousers that came down over the knees to her calves like short jodhpurs, she might be any blurting, restless Western girl.

In Shiraz one lives in the scent of stock and cypress and magnolia. In the oldest of the mosques one notices that, with a gay lack of Moslem orthodoxy, the tulip, the rose, and the nightingale have been introduced as motifs in the tiles.

You will be told a hundred times that this is the town of the poet Hafiz, and you will visit his tomb in its little garden. Persian visitors stand there murmuring lines of his verses or the prayer inscribed on the tomb. The superstitious bring a volume of his poems and, opening it at random, with eyes closed, put a finger on a line, open their eyes, and get their guidance. My schoolmaster swore by it; a line of Hafiz, he said, was responsible for his second marriage.

More than 70 per cent of the Iranian people are said to be illiterate, but the oral tradition is strong, and I doubt if there is a single person in Shiraz who could not recite a poem by Hafiz or indeed by two even earlier great poets of Iran—Saadi and Firdausi. The taxi driver could; so could the thin, unhappy waiter. The student who had met me sat on my balcony and, enlivened by a glass of Pepsi-Cola (for he was a strict Moslem and would not drink alcohol), declaimed Hafiz to me, rolling out the splendid Arabic words that are interspersed with the

233

Persian. In revenge I read back a nineteenth-century English translation to him. The prestige of Omar Khayyám is low. They can't understand what FitzGerald saw in him.

Later we went off to mortify our bodies and our knee joints by taking tea with some dervishes in their retreat. We entered a dusty, neglected garden and, in a stone room bare except for the carpet, we took off our shoes and squatted in agony with a dozen dervishes, not all elderly, who sat by their samovar and gently gave us glasses of tea. They handed around a pipe to puff and spoke to us amiably of the vanity of human possessions and the desires of this world and of the necessity of contemplating death and attaining a mystical union with the divine—a state of mind the poet Hafiz sought by drinking the indifferent wine of the country and sublimating the distress of his love affairs. Hafiz and Khayyám both overrated the Persian grape.

In the middle of our chat, the sound of a heart-rending, groaning chant came from the room beyond us, where other dervishes were in prayer. The appalling sound, like the moan of a cow parted from its calf, was taken up by our friends. They rocked on their haunches and raised their eyes to heaven at the mention of the sacred name of Allah, and then suddenly took up conversation again as if nothing had happened.

One or two of these dervishes were married and had left their wives and families for three or four years in order to meditate. Quite a few people from Shiraz come and sit with the dervishes on Fridays and meditate for the day. It is a therapy. In Turkey, Kemal Atatürk suppressed the

dervishes; the Persians, more tolerant by nature, give freedom to the dervishes, as they do without a second thought
to Jews, Armenians, or any religious group; outside the
Lebanon, Iran must be the least fanatical country in the
Middle East.

We left the dervishes for the teahouse and the hubble-
bubble pipe.

There is the brown, burned-up Persia and there is the
green country by the Caspian Sea. Green Persia begins the
other side of the Elburz Mountains north of Tehran. I
went north by train, a smart diesel this time, across the
800-mile Persian desert. The sand blows in, fills your
eyes, nose, and throat, and puts a film of grit on everything. The dining car, full of high-ranking army officers,
is luxurious. The train dies in long silences at village
stations, dogs sniff at the wheels, a camel crosses the tracks.

After several hours, you rise into a region of high, fantastic rock. At 8,000 feet the train moves around the
outside of the mountains, through scores of tunnels, and
along precipices. It comes down in terraces and runs across
a spectacular viaduct, 500 feet above the valley, to the next
range, and then sweeps down into the gorge. At either end
of the mountains, east and west, is the barbed wire of the
Russian frontier.

The air is moist and warm. The olive trees, the orange
groves, the pasturage, rice fields, and tea plantations lie
beside wide, fast coppery rivers pouring over shingle beds
toward the Caspian Sea. The fortified mud-wall villages
have gone. Here the houses are white or blue, often timber-

fronted and often two or three storeys high, and they are not only in open villages of long streets. There are houses scattered singly over the countryside—a thing unheard of in the south.

There is the sense of potential wealth here, of people who divide their lives between agriculture and the sea. There are crowds at the country stations. We got out at Chalus and were beset by dozens of men, women, and children selling reed brushes and brooms, as if the first need of a traveller was to sweep up somebody's house, and by the usual beggars and herb sellers. The cars waiting there are usually newish, but with fenders and sides bashed in by collisions. Half a mile out of Chalus, as we drove fast over the rough dusty roads, a large flint flew up from the road and smashed our windshield. Then I noticed that the glass of nearly every passing car was smashed. We drove on with the glass in our laps and our fingers bleeding, passing the donkey-loads of grasses and rushes that were coming home.

All Persians who can afford it send their families for months out of the heat of the tableland to the soft beaches of the Caspian. There are smart little resorts, and at Ramsar, where the Shah has a country estate, the hotels are luxurious and there is a casino. The country was hot and rich, and in April the air was honeyed with the scent of wisteria. Girls with beautiful eyes walked by with branches of wisteria in their hands.

The highlands of Persia are a strain on the nerves, the altitude depresses the spirits, the space and poverty weary the eye; but here, along the Caspian coast, the Westerner is filled with voluptuous emotions and is more at home.

The towns and villages seem less Eastern and more Russian. When I said this to my Persian friends, they were offended and firmly explained to me that southern Russia was "very Persian." The Russians, in their century-and-a-half quarrel with the Persians, have in fact taken over some of the Persian provinces. But I was thinking of those wooden villas and town halls with wooden classical columns in the façades, painted turquoise blue, with fine windows and the fantastically cut, toylike metal decorations on the eaves and dormers.

Some of the women in the Caspian provinces wear the *chadar*. I called on a general and landowner who had a villa between Ramsar and Pahlevi, and he stopped to say a few words to two or three women as they passed us in a field, and admired the baby one of them was carrying. She drew the *chadar* across her face, looked aside with lowered eyes, and showed no sign of hearing the compliment. She was behaving according to polite custom. But most of the women are unveiled. They wear a spotted red or blue dress over their pyjama-like trousers, a broad tartan apron or stomacher, small black-and-white hats, flat and solid, for carrying their tins or jars of water or sacks of grain, and a white veil behind the head. They are short, sharp-faced, bright-eyed, often very pretty, and they lean forward from the hips as if this were their manner of resting: they almost always have a load on their backs or heads. It is usually the women who are hoeing in the tea gardens. They hack away silently in groups at an extraordinary speed. They march down from the hills with long mountaineer strides, five or six of them at a time, chattering and laughing. They have brought in their jars of yogurt to the market and go back with cloth or a large fish.

But to go back to the general, I found him reading Montgomery's *Memoirs*. He had the military man's passion for organization and "betterment." He had bought a small, barren estate by the sea on the way to Pahlevi and had turned it into fine orange and olive groves and tea gardens. Angry about the state of Iranian politics, out of favour in Tehran, he had retired to show, in a small way, how the standards of agriculture could be raised. A handsome, cultivated man, he was in deep trouble with the peasantry and the politicians, neither of whom like new methods. He called them "the clowns." He was a reserved man, a benevolent aristocrat, a man of boundless friendship, but stern with his children: "They must repay to Iran what they have learned in Europe. Knowledge is not for amusement."

The general was rich; but the next day I spent some time with a workman who had a large wooden house in Pahlevi and a country bungalow outside the town. The bungalow was surrounded by poplars and a fence of rushes; there he grew his broad beans, his runner beans, his garlic. This man was a working fitter in the shipyard at Pahlevi. We sat out on the porch. His son, the headmaster of the high school, sat beside his father, who had built the structure with his own hands and installed his own electric light and water pump. They ordered vodka for me, but the father—a strict Moslem—would not touch it; nor would he smoke; and, in the presence of his father, the forty-

year-old son would not dare to drink or smoke. We ate
our garlic and our radishes in the soft, warm, damp evening
air. But for the gnats it was very restful, like a scene from
Chekhov. We talked about hunting, for the father was a
crack shot; on the Caspian, people go for miles along the
beaches after wild duck.

Fathers are despots in Persia, but the real struggle between this father and his son was not about smoking and
drinking; it was the struggle between custom and the modern, Western world that was breaking in, the struggle
between old and new. "I will not go to my daughter-in-
law's house," the old workman said. "They have complained that I eat with my fingers."

Pahlevi is the caviar port of the Caspian. It is a pretty,
prosperous town of fishermen who toil at putting out their
quarter of a mile of net into the sea and then, in shouting
teams thirty strong, haul it in. This is one of the sights of
the town. The State has only lately installed a mechanical
capstan. Sturgeon and what they call whitefish, a kind of
sea bass, are their favourite catch. Muffled in Russian-
styled clothes, the men in the sturgeon trade work in the
cold-storage plant where thousands of frozen sturgeon and
small yawning whales are stacked—an awful death house.
But you are fed on the best caviar in the world, the grey-
green oily kind, in the laboratories; and they are breeding
sturgeon by artificial means now. A rich American market
has opened up for Pahlevi, but most of its caviar and fish
goes to Russia.

My weekend with my schoolmaster's friends and relations was marred for me only by the reckless hunting habits of my hosts, who drove along the beaches shooting falcons, sea gulls, and teal in an undiscriminating slaughter and, when we got home, let their young children play with the wounded birds. There is a savage side to life in this country, but it is not altogether the fault of the Persians. After the war they learned from American and British troops to hunt gazelles from jeeps and to kill anything at sight. In a few years the automobile has destroyed the ancient skill, the grace and art, of the Persian chase.

When I was in the south I drove out from Shiraz to the ruins of Persepolis. They are the Persian, indeed the Aryan, foundation. This was the spiritual centre of the ancient world empire of Artaxerxes and Darius; Babylon and the Greek colonies fell to it, and at one time the Persians were on the Danube. To the Greeks the Persians were, like all foreigners, barbarians, yet in administration and tolerance the Persians certainly surpassed the Greeks. Alexander the Great destroyed the great palaces of Persepolis; this was his revenge for the burning of Athens. Today, to stand on the great stone platforms of this fantastic ruin, under its heavy arches, is one of the great emotional moments of travel in Iran. The ruin is highly placed, so that from it one surveys a wide valley. Its tombs, cut high in the rock, convey a sense of great power.

Persepolis stands by the roadside, one of those main roads that traverse the country, and after the sombre marvel of the site, it is this road that remains in the mind. This country is a road. It is a road that has seen empire after empire, kingdom after kingdom, because it is a road that first offered itself to the outsider and then detained and cultivated him. It is a road that has been a meeting ground and, eventually, an island of civilization in which we can, in an obscure yet real way, recognize things connected with our own.

A NOTE ON THE TYPE

THE TEXT of this book was set on the Linotype in *Janson*, a recutting made direct from type cast from matrices long thought to have been made by the Dutchman Anton Janson, who was a practicing type founder in Leipzig during the years 1668–87. However, it has been conclusively demonstrated that these types are actually the work of Nicholas Kis (1650–1702), a Hungarian, who most probably learned his trade from the master Dutch type founder Dirk Voskens. The type is an excellent example of the influential and sturdy Dutch types that prevailed in England up to the time William Caslon developed his own incomparable designs from these Dutch faces.

Composed, printed, and bound by
The Haddon Craftsmen, Inc., Scranton, Pa.
Typography and binding design
based on originals by Warren Chappell

A NOTE ABOUT THE AUTHOR

V(ICTOR) S(AWDON) PRITCHETT was born in Ipswich, England, in 1900. He attended Alleyn's School (London). After working in the leather trade and as a commercial traveler and shop assistant in France, he set up as a newspaper correspondent there, in Spain, and in Morocco. Mr. Pritchett later turned his attention to criticism, the novel, and short stories. Following World War II, he was literary editor of the *New Statesman and Nation*. He is now a regular contributor of stories and articles to British and American magazines and to *The New York Times Book Review*. He is perhaps best known here for *The Spanish Temper* (1954), *The Living Novel* and other books of criticism, and his collections of short stories, *The Sailor, Sense of Humour, and Other Stories* (1956) and *When My Girl Comes Home* (1961). He is married to a charming Welsh lady, has two children, and lives in London.

June 1964